Balboa Press books may be ordered through booksellers or by contacting:

Balboa Press
A Division of Hay House
1663 Liberty Drive
Bloomington, IN 47403
www.balboapress.com
844-682-1282

Because of the dynamic nature of the Internet, any web addresses or links contained in this book may have changed since publication and may no longer be valid. The views expressed in this work are solely those of the author and do not necessarily reflect the views of the publisher, and the publisher hereby disclaims any responsibility for them.

The author of this book does not dispense medical advice or prescribe the use of any technique as a form of treatment for physical, emotional, or medical problems without the advice of a physician, either directly or indirectly. The intent of the author is only to offer information of a general nature to help you in your quest for emotional and spiritual well-being. In the event you use any of the information in this book for yourself, which is your constitutional right, the author and the publisher assume no responsibility for your actions.

Any people depicted in stock imagery provided by Getty Images are models,
and such images are being used for illustrative purposes only.
Certain stock imagery © Getty Images.

ISBN: 979-8-7652-2957-6 (sc)
ISBN: 979-8-7652-2956-9 (e)

Print information available on the last page.

Balboa Press rev. date: 06/24/2022

Presents

DAILY PLANNING SYSTEM

FOR COLLEGE COACHES

by Mandy Green

Published by

Busy Coach

© 2022 Mandy Green Busy Coach, LLC.

Cover design by Alex Novik, www.branding.city

A DIVISION OF HAY HOUSE

Visit us on the web at:

www.busy.coach

Or, for more information email me at:

mandy@busy.coach

This portfolio is the property of:

Name: _____

Home Address: _____

City, State, Zip: _____

School Name: _____

School Address: _____

Cell Phone: _____

Office Phone: _____

E-mail: _____

In case of an emergency, please contact:

Name: _____

Cell Phone: _____   Office Phone: _____

Busy Coach

Youngstown, OH 44514

RECRUITING OPPORTUNITIES

JANUARY 2022						
						1
2	3	4	5	6	7	8
9	10	11	12	13	14	15
16	17	18	19	20	21	22
23	24	25	26	27	28	29
30	31					

FEBRUARY 2022						
	1	2	3	4	5	
6	7	8	9	10	11	12
13	14	15	16	17	18	19
20	21	22	23	24	25	26
27	28					

MARCH 2022						
	1	2	3	4	5	
6	7	8	9	10	11	12
13	14	15	16	17	18	19
20	21	22	23	24	25	26
27	28	29	30	31		

APRIL 2022						
					1	2
3	4	5	6	7	8	9
10	11	12	13	14	15	16
17	18	19	20	21	22	23
24	25	26	27	28	29	30

MAY 2022						
1	2	3	4	5	6	7
8	9	10	11	12	13	14
15	16	17	18	19	20	21
22	23	24	25	26	27	28
29	30	31				

JUNE 2022						
			1	2	3	4
5	6	7	8	9	10	11
12	13	14	15	16	17	18
19	20	21	22	23	24	25
26	27	28	29	30		

JULY 2022						
					1	2
3	4	5	6	7	8	9
10	11	12	13	14	15	16
17	18	19	20	21	22	23
24	25	26	27	28	29	30
31						

AUGUST 2022						
	1	2	3	4	5	6
7	8	9	10	11	12	13
14	15	16	17	18	19	20
21	22	23	24	25	26	27
28	29	30	31			

SEPTEMBER 2022						
				1	2	3
4	5	6	7	8	9	10
11	12	13	14	15	16	17
18	19	20	21	22	23	24
25	26	27	28	29	30	

OCTOBER 2022						
						1
2	3	4	5	6	7	8
9	10	11	12	13	14	15
16	17	18	19	20	21	22
23	24	25	26	27	28	29
30	31					

NOVEMBER 2022						
	1	2	3	4	5	
6	7	8	9	10	11	12
13	14	15	16	17	18	19
20	21	22	23	24	25	26
27	28	29	30	31		

DECEMBER 2022						
				1	2	3
4	5	6	7	8	9	10
11	12	13	14	15	16	17
18	19	20	21	22	23	24
25	26	27	28	29	30	31

JANUARY 2023						
1	2	3	4	5	6	7
8	9	10	11	12	13	14
15	16	17	18	19	20	21
22	23	24	25	26	27	28
29	30	31				

FEBRUARY 2023						
			1	2	3	4
5	6	7	8	9	10	11
12	13	14	15	16	17	18
19	20	21	22	23	24	25
26	27	28				

MARCH 2023						
			1	2	3	4
5	6	7	8	9	10	11
12	13	14	15	16	17	18
19	20	21	22	23	24	25
26	27	28	29	30	31	

APRIL 2023						
						1
2	3	4	5	6	7	8
9	10	11	12	13	14	15
16	17	18	19	20	21	22
23	24	25	26	27	28	29
30						

MAY 2023						
	1	2	3	4	5	6
7	8	9	10	11	12	13
14	15	16	17	18	19	20
21	22	23	24	25	26	27
28	29	30	31			

JUNE 2023						
				1	2	3
4	5	6	7	8	9	10
11	12	13	14	15	16	17
18	19	20	21	22	23	24
25	26	27	28	29	30	

JULY 2023						
						1
2	3	4	5	6	7	8
9	10	11	12	13	14	15
16	17	18	19	20	21	22
23	24	25	26	27	28	29
30	31					

AUGUST 2023						
		1	2	3	4	5
6	7	8	9	10	11	12
13	14	15	16	17	18	19
20	21	22	23	24	25	26
27	28	29	30	31		

SEPTEMBER 2023						
					1	2
3	4	5	6	7	8	9
10	11	12	13	14	15	16
17	18	19	20	21	22	23
24	25	26	27	28	29	30

OCTOBER 2023						
1	2	3	4	5	6	7
8	9	10	11	12	13	14
15	16	17	18	19	20	21
22	23	24	25	26	27	28
29	30	31				

NOVEMBER 2023						
			1	2	3	4
5	6	7	8	9	10	11
12	13	14	15	16	17	18
19	20	21	22	23	24	25
26	27	28	29	30		

DECEMBER 2023						
					1	2
3	4	5	6	7	8	9
10	11	12	13	14	15	16
17	18	19	20	21	22	23
24	25	26	27	28	29	30
31						

JANUARY 2024						
	1	2	3	4	5	6
7	8	9	10	11	12	13
14	15	16	17	18	19	20
21	22	23	24	25	26	27
28	29	30	31			

FEBRUARY 2024						
				1	2	3
4	5	6	7	8	9	10
11	12	13	14	15	16	17
18	19	20	21	22	23	24
25	26	27	28			

MARCH 2024						
					1	2
3	4	5	6	7	8	9
10	11	12	13	14	15	16
17	18	19	20	21	22	23
24	25	26	27	28	29	30
31						

APRIL 2024						
	1	2	3	4	5	6
7	8	9	10	11	12	13
14	15	16	17	18	19	20
21	22	23	24	25	26	27
28	29	30				

MAY 2024						
		1	2	3	4	
5	6	7	8	9	10	11
12	13	14	15	16	17	18
19	20	21	22	23	24	25
26	27	28	29	30	31	

JUNE 2024						
						1
2	3	4	5	6	7	8
9	10	11	12	13	14	15
16	17	18	19	20	21	22
23	24	25	26	27	28	29
30						

JULY 2024						
	1	2	3	4	5	6
7	8	9	10	11	12	13
14	15	16	17	18	19	20
21	22	23	24	25	26	27
28	29	30	31			

AUGUST 2024						
				1	2	3
4	5	6	7	8	9	10
11	12	13	14	15	16	17
18	19	20	21	22	23	24
25	26	27	28	29	30	31

How to Use Your Daily Planning System

Coach, as you know, a huge part of our job as college coaches is to win on game day. Everyone tries to win game days. But as you also know, most days are for practice, recruiting, and office work.

The key to success on game day is winning those Mondays, Tuesdays, Wednesdays, Thursdays and Fridays when we are in the office. The only thing we can control is today. So it's crucial to have a written ongoing plan to keep you on track, that stays within reach and states what you intend to accomplish every day.

Results-getting performances on and off of the field of play boil down to better day by day execution.

Your ability as a coach to think, work, and create faster, smarter, and with a more innovative edge will differentiate you from your competition. Yes, you need to work hard to get the results you want, but when you take the time to plan, prioritize, and organize, you will be working smarter than most of your competitors, which will lead to better results and in the long run you will save yourself a lot of wasted time and energy.

As a college coach myself for over 23 years now, I know how hard it can be to keep track of all the tasks that you need to do each day, week, and month.

Coaches say that staying focused is a huge challenge. So it's crucial to have an ongoing plan to keep you on track, a written outline that stays within reach and states what you intend to accomplish every day.

Since there is nothing out there specifically for what we do to help with daily work execution as college coaches, I created this first-ever time management tool for Coaches that gives you everything you need to reach higher levels of performance, prioritize high value activities, take daily steps to accomplish your goals, and manage your time more effectively.

This planner is designed for coaches who want to reach higher levels of performance in the office by improving their recruiting effectiveness, personal organization, and personal productivity.

The planner will provide a system of prompts and questions that will help you focus on your most important projects and core tasks, and to implement and record important information.

To get the results you want, every day you need to be taking action in order to move forward with your program, and the planner will help you do this. This day planner page gets you focused on the projects that you want to complete or move forward with for that day and the core tasks that will help you achieve it. This planner will also help you schedule your day with more structure so you can help reduce the chaos, for at least parts of the day.

As you get into the routine of planning out your day and recording metrics and statistics, you will see that your **program will become more productive and less chaotic.** By taking consistent action, you are putting the steps in place to grow and build a successful program.

It's simple, Productivity (Time Management + Prioritization) = Next Level Results.

As you dig into this planner, please don't hesitate to reach out if you have any questions to mandy@busy.coach.

Get after it and good luck!

To your success,
Mandy Green

Start Here

To help you maximize this powerful tool, I've created detailed video tutorials on how to use all of the different frameworks you'll find inside. Don't miss those. You can find them at https://mandy-green.mykajabi.com/library. For now, here are some basic instructions.

1. Begin by taking the quick assessment on page 8 so we can create a baseline of where we are starting. The goal of this assessment is to help you identify areas for improvement in the major areas of your coaching life.

2. On page 10 you will establish your vision for the year. Think big. Where would you like to see your program, team, career, or life at the end of the year?

3. Then break down your vision into seven to ten annual goals on page 11. A quick daily review of these will keep them visible and fresh all year long.

4. On page 10-11 is where you will create your battle board. This is a visual board where you can start planning month by month what you are going to be working towards and start setting deadlines for when you will be accomplishing your goals and metrics you have set.

5. Next, on page 12-13 you will break your annual goals into smaller chunks that you will focus on over the next 3 months. A daily review of these will ensure you stay motivated and clear on the next steps for completion.

6. On page 14-15, you will establish what your morning and evening rituals will be. These will be a work in progress but are vitally important to your success in winning with your execution day by day.

7. Page 16-23 is where you will learn how to fill out the daily execution system.

8. Page 24-25 is for setting your monthly focus. Use this section at the beginning of every month to drive the direction of your month, week, and day to eliminate activities that just do NOT fit in.

9. Page 26-27 is for you to set up your ideal week. If you don't carve out the time for what matters most at home, for yourself, or for the high value activities in your program, they tend to get pushed out by other fires that happen. We are not going to let that happen anymore!!

10. You have 90 days worth of planning pages to use.

11. On page 90-91, you will see an end of the month review. As you know, game film doesn't lie. You watch the film after you compete to see what parts of the game plan were executed well and what wasn't done well so you can figure out what adjustments you need to make. I want you to go through the same process to self evaluate on the progress you made throughout the course of the month. Go back through the month to evaluate the tasks you chose to work on and see if it matches up with the results that you got.

COACHING ASSESSMENT

Before we get to taking action on your goals, let's create a baseline of where we are starting. The goal of this assessment is to help you identify areas for improvement in the major areas of your coaching life. As with any self-assessment, the goal isn't a complete snapshot of every nuance of your life, but rather a good opportunity for overall self-reflection. Don't worry about the exact wording of these descriptions. Instead, just give your overall impression of how you rate in each category based on the past 30 days.

HEALTH
I regularly take care of myself so that I can feel my best. I want my overall physical and emotional health to be optimized to make me feel energetic and strong each day. I strive to eat well, sleep well, and work out so that I have the physical energy and stamina to consistently bring my best, enjoy life, and deal with its challenges.   1 2 3 4 5 6 7 8 9 10

MENTAL/EMOTIONAL
I keep a positive outlook and attitude. I take care of myself by being mindful to the energy, focus, and emotions I really want to experience and generate in life. 1 2 3 4 5 6 7 8 9 10

FAMILY
I am present with my family when I am able to be home with them. I am creating deep connection, and fun and positive energy with the family members that I keep in contact with. It's evident that I love my family and I'm doing my best for them.   1 2 3 4 5 6 7 8 9 10

FRIENDS/LIFESTYLE
I have hobbies outside of work that I enjoy and take part in a few times a week. My immediate social circle of friends bring connection, fun, and positive energy into my life. I seek out positive people and I do my best to bring positive energy and real authenticity into all of my relationships.   1 2 3 4 5 6 7 8 9 10

COACHING
I feel clear, energized, and fulfilled by my work and contributions to my team, staff, and program. I believe my work or day's effort adds real value and is a true reflection of my best efforts and contributions. I am truly engaged and excited by what I'm doing.   1 2 3 4 5 6 7 8 9 10

RECRUITING
I have a plan for how to effectively and efficiently recruiting this generation of recruits, their parents and club coaches. I am confident in selling myself, my team, program, and school. I carve out time every single week to work on recruiting and make sure I am prioritizing high value tasks vs getting stuck doing low value tasks.   1 2 3 4 5 6 7 8 9 10

ADMINISTRATION
I have set up a high performance environment with yearly, quarterly, monthly, weekly, and daily methods of operation. I have systems in place to automate, delegate, or delete all routine tasks.   1 2 3 4 5 6 7 8 9 10

TEAM/STAFF
We have a strong vision, strong leadership, and a strong culture. I am surrounded by people who I enjoy being around everyday.   1 2 3 4 5 6 7 8 9 10

PRODUCTIVITY
I am successfully completing sequential steps in a timely manner that bring me closer to accomplishing important tasks, projects, or goals I have set. I am able to stay on task and still make progress even when I feel unmotivated, distracted or discouraged.   1 2 3 4 5 6 7 8 9 10

IDEAS TO IMPROVE ANY OF THESE AREAS INCLUDE:

TOTAL SCORE:_____

You have a lot of people counting on your to bring you're "A" game every day! Let's get to work!!

- Mandy Green

VISION FOR THE YEAR

Where I'd like to be at the end of this year, what I'd like to achieve, what impact I'd like to have created...

month: i.e.., when are you wrapping up recruiting?

Create your 'Battle Board'

Looking at this every day will help keep you focused, motivated and accountable to your big goals. When are you wrapping up your recruiting? What metrics do you want to hit? What recruiting events do you have? Projects you're focused on? When are you having camps? When do you want to focus on bringing in campus visits?

MONTH

S	M	T	W	T	F	S

MONTH

S	M	T	W	T	F	S

MONTH

S	M	T	W	T	F	S

MONTH

S	M	T	W	T	F	S

MONTH

S	M	T	W	T	F	S

MONTH

S	M	T	W	T	F	S

GOALS FOR THE YEAR

What Recruiting, Team, Administration, or Personal Goals you want to have achieved by the end of the year...

Don't be guilty of looking at your phone more than you're looking at your goals. Map out what you are going to be achieving each month.

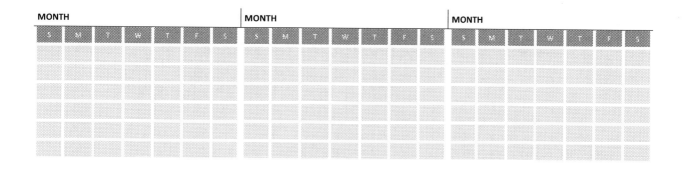

SMALLER GOAL TO FOCUS ON IN THE NEXT 12 WEEKS

Team Goal	Recruiting Goal

Step 1: Identify Your Goals

Step 2: My Benefits to Reaching this Goal

Step 3: Major Obstacles and Mountains to Climb to Reach this Goal

Step 4: Skills or Knowledge Required to Reach this Goal

Step 5: Plan of Action to Reach this Goal

Step 6: Completion Dates

Step 7: Streak Tracker Every day you spend time working on this goal, check off your progress.

1	2	3	4	5	6	7	8	9	10		1	2	3	4	5	6	7	8	9	10
11	12	13	14	15	16	17	18	19	20		11	12	13	14	15	16	17	18	19	20
21	22	23	24	25	26	27	28	29	30		21	22	23	24	25	26	27	28	29	30
31	32	33	34	35	36	37	38	39	40		31	32	33	34	35	36	37	38	39	40
41	42	43	44	45	46	47	48	49	50		41	42	43	44	45	46	47	48	49	50
51	52	53	54	55	56	57	58	59	60		51	52	53	54	55	56	57	58	59	60
61	62	63	64	65	66	67	68	69	70		61	62	63	64	65	66	67	68	69	70
71	72	73	74	75	76	77	78	79	80		71	72	73	74	75	76	77	78	79	80
81	82	83	84	85	86	87	88	89	90		81	82	83	84	85	86	87	88	89	90

SMALLER GOAL TO FOCUS ON IN THE NEXT 12 WEEKS

Administrative Goal	Personal Goal
Step 1: Identify Your Goals	
Step 2: My Benefits to Reaching this Goal	
Step 3: Major Obstacles and Mountains to Climb to Reach this Goal	
Step 4: Skills or Knowledge Required to Reach this Goal	
Step 5: Plan of Action to Reach this Goal	
Step 6: Completion Dates	

Step 7: Streak Tracker Every day you spend time working on this goal, check off your progress.

1	2	3	4	5	6	7	8	9	10	1	2	3	4	5	6	7	8	9	10
11	12	13	14	15	16	17	18	19	20	11	12	13	14	15	16	17	18	19	20
21	22	23	24	25	26	27	28	29	30	21	22	23	24	25	26	27	28	29	30
31	32	33	34	35	36	37	38	39	40	31	32	33	34	35	36	37	38	39	40
41	42	43	44	45	46	47	48	49	50	41	42	43	44	45	46	47	48	49	50
51	52	53	54	55	56	57	58	59	60	51	52	53	54	55	56	57	58	59	60
61	62	63	64	65	66	67	68	69	70	61	62	63	64	65	66	67	68	69	70
71	72	73	74	75	76	77	78	79	80	71	72	73	74	75	76	77	78	79	80
81	82	83	84	85	86	87	88	89	90	81	82	83	84	85	86	87	88	89	90

DAILY POWER UP AND POWER DOWN RITUALS

	MORNING POWER UP RITUAL	TOTAL TIME
	List your ritual activities and necessary time for completion	

	Activity	Tie Allotted
1		
2		
3		
4		
5		
6		
7		
8		
9		
10		

	WORK DAY START UP RITUAL	TOTAL TIME
	List your ritual activities and necessary time for completion	

	Activity	Tie Allotted
1		
2		
3		
4		
5		
6		
7		
8		
9		
10		

WORK DAY SHUTDOWN RITUAL

		TOTAL TIME
List your ritual activities and necessary time for completion		
	Activity	Tie Allotted
1		
2		
3		
4		
5		
6		
7		
8		
9		
10		

EVENING POWER DOWN RITUAL

		TOTAL TIME
List your ritual activities and necessary time for completion		
	Activity	Tie Allotted
1		
2		
3		
4		
5		
6		
7		
8		
9		
10		

HOW TO FILL OUT THE DAILY EXECUTION PAGE

As you begin to use your Busy Coach Game Plan, invest some time to better understand several important features of the calendar. The following steps will help you use your Productivity Planner more effectively

Your Busy Coach Game Plan Execution Page is there to work for YOU. There is no right way to fill in this page. I don't want you to feel overwhelmed by having to fill spaces or sections in 'correctly'. Plan your day in a way that feels the best for you and use the planning page to prompt you as you go along.

Start The Night Before

I recommend that you plan your day the night before. This way, you can get a good night's sleep and when you wake up in the morning, you will be able to start your day knowing exactly what to do.

Also, the best morning routines start out the night before as well. Lay your clothes out the night before, pack lunches, make sure your bag is packed, so you don't have to think about what you need in the morning. Your day can get off to a great start if you've planned out your start.

Pregame planning

In all of the research that I have done about what makes successful people different than the rest, it seems that successful people take advantage of the first few minutes of their workday to get grounded and focused. Once you've adopted the right mindset and routine for success, the rest of the day flows much more smoothly.

When you do wake up in the morning, take out your daily planning page. Dedicate 10-20 minutes of quiet time and solitude each morning to pause and think about what matters most today. Strategize, write down the major outcomes you want to accomplish and the core tasks that will help you achieve it, delegate and divide tasks.

DAILY THEME

Your daily theme is a simple way of creating an organizing principle for each of your days. As a college coach your bombarded with responsibilities—having a 'Daily Theme' is a way of creating a 'decision filter', so you can quickly plan, organize and schedule your week. I.E.:

Monday's - Administrative Tasks, Tuesday's - Recruiting, Wednesday's - Team, Thursday's - Meetings, Friday's - Catch-up, Saturday's - Rest, Sunday's - Personal Growth

Theming your days tells you what the core idea of your day is all about. You can also theme your day, based on the projects you're working on too. The main benefit is to reduce the amount of decisions you need to make in a day. Daily Theme's are a simple and powerful tool to keep you sane and focused.

DAY: _____   DAILY THEME:

Win the Day Planning

Today, I am grateful I get to be a coach because:

I have reviewed my team, recruiting, administrative & personal goals ☐

Today's Results List: List in priority order the top 3 things you can accomplish that would make a measurable impact on your goals and projects? What metric are you trying to hit? Schedule it.

Priority #1:   **Metric I am aiming for_____**

Priority #2:   **Metric I am aiming for_____**

Priority #3:   **Metric I am aiming for_____**

○ **Morning Routine**   ○ **Workday Startup Routine**

TIME	DAILY SCHEDULE
5 am	
6 am	
7 am	
8 am	
9 am	
10 am	
11 am	
12 pm	
1 pm	
2 pm	
3 pm	
4 pm	
5 pm	
6 pm	
7 pm	
8 pm	
9 pm	
10 pm	
11 pm	

○ **Workday Shutdown Routine**   ○ **Evening Routine**

Person/People I need to Lead or Connect with Today (and How to Do It Well)

What or Who Am I Waiting On To Get a Project Done:

Who Needs Something From Me Today or This Week That I Can Proactively Get To Them?

Staff meeting topics to cover:

Team meeting topics to cover:

HOW TO FILL OUT THE DAILY EXECUTION PAGE

WIN THE DAY WITH A GREAT MORNING ROUTINE

Morning Routine– Refer to page 20 where you will establish and map out your morning routine. Check the box if you accomplished your morning routine.

Morning Startup Routine– Refer to page 20 where you will establish and map out your morning startup routine. Check the box if you accomplished your morning start-up routine.

GRATITUDE

Take a moment to be grateful: Identify at least one thing you're grateful for. You can express gratitude for something personal or it can be program/staff/team-related

Why gratitude? The act of writing out our gratitude for even 5 minutes in the morning helps to shift our focus from what we don't have to what we do have. Expressing your gratitude for something is very motivational and reminds us to put small things into perspective.

REVIEW GOALS AND TODAY'S FOCUS

This area answer's the question: "What's the 1-3 things you could accomplish that would make a measurable impact on your goals and projects?". Too often a day gets 'away on us' and we forget the big things we're working towards. You need to constantly be reminding yourself of what you are trying to accomplish goal wise so you don't get too far off track. If you can block off and tackle even one of these vital tasks, the compounding daily effect of doing this day after day will be immeasurable.

After doing a quick review of your goals, list the top three most important tasks for the day, and commit to getting these tasks done first.

Line-up your time to make that happen. Set aside 25-90 minute blocks of time each day, one for each of three key tasks you must accomplish. Set up these blocks of time when your energy and creativity are the best. When you are the most focused and when you will get interrupted the least.

Contemporary productivity gurus, such as Robin Sharma, recommend you "spend the first 90 minutes of your day on your number one priority." That's the 80-20 rule. Ninety minutes is about 20% of your day, and concentrated effort on your number one priority at this time will give you 80% of your results for the day. Those are rough numbers of course. But in all likelihood you will find the first morning hours will be the only time of day you are able to focus on priority projects without interruption.

Knowing the top three things that you need to accomplish in a day gives you extra focus and helps you stay on task when you arrive at the office.

KEY METRICS

It is also important for coaches to measure the metrics to see how successful they are and what impact they are having. The metrics you measure will depend entirely on your program and what projects you want to undertake. For example, how many phone calls are you going to make? How many campus visits are you going to schedule? How much time are you going to spend returning recruiting emails? Set your metric and then work like crazy to hit your numbers day by day.

Win the Day Planning

Today, I am grateful I get to be a coach because: 3

4

I have reviewed my team, recruiting, administrative & personal goals ☐

Today's Results List: List in priority order the top 3 things you can accomplish that would make a measurable impact on your goals and projects? What metric are you trying to hit? Schedule it.

Priority #1:   **Metric I am aiming for_____**

Priority #2:   **Metric I am aiming for_____**

Priority #3:   **Metric I am aiming for_____**

○ **Morning Routine**   ○ **Workday Startup Routine**

TIME	DAILY SCHEDULE
5 am	
6 am	
7 am	
8 am	
9 am	
10 am	
11 am	
12 pm	
1 pm	
2 pm	
3 pm	
4 pm	
5 pm	
6 pm	
7 pm	
8 pm	
9 pm	
10 pm	
11 pm	

○ **Workday Shutdown Routine**   ○ **Evening Routine**

Person/People I need to Lead or Connect with Today (and How to Do It Well)

Staff meeting topics to cover:

What or Who Am I Waiting On To Get a Project Done:

Team meeting topics to cover:

Who Needs Something From Me Today or This Week That I Can Proactively Get To Them?

HOW TO FILL OUT THE DAILY EXECUTION PAGE

3 DAILY QUESTIONS

1. **Person/People I need to Lead or Connect with Today (and How to Do It Well)**. For example, what club coach can I reach out to today and develop a better relationship with that could potentially help me with recruiting quality student-athletes to my program? Or, what person on campus could I reach out to today to introduce myself or to thank them for helping me with something?

2. **What or Who Am I Waiting On To Get a Project Done:** Take a look at your to-do list. What information will you need to get from somebody to complete the task. Reach out at the beginning of the day to give them time to get you what you need. Don't wait until the fire happens.

3. **Who Needs Something From Me Today or This Week Thant I Can Proactively Get To Them?** Again, don't wait until the fire happens. Think ahead. Who is going to need something from you this coming week that you can proactively get to them before they even ask for it.

Hourly schedule

Use this space to record meetings, practices, workouts, appointments, lunch dates, etc., here. Also use it to block out time needed to complete high priority activities that will help you reach your goals.   If high priority activities don't get scheduled, the probably won't get done: Or if they do get done, they won't be done well.   Schedule time daily to send emails, plan practice, do administrative work, return phone calls, recruit, manage your team, meet with staff, etc. These activities should be clearly blocked into your schedule at 15-minute, half-hour, or hour-long time slots, depending on how long each task should take you.

***Please Note: These aren't hard rules for how you HAVE TO work your day. They're principles to keep you grounded in knowing where you're investing your time and the activities you've chosen to spend your time on.

STAFF AND TEAM MEETING TOPICS

Use this space to jot down any thoughts you have or key points you will want to hit in any team or staff meetings that you have for the day.

WORKDAY AND EVENING ROUTINES

Work Day Shutdown Routine-You will establish these on page 21. This is what you do as you prepare to leave the office and transition into the evening. This should include what you need to do to wrap up your day, and enable you to hit the ground running tomorrow. Again, estimate how much time you expect each activity to take and then write down the total.

Evening Routine– You will establish this on page 21. This is what you do right before you go to bed in the evening. This should be anything that sets you up for a restful night but also could be things that are going to help you win the day tomorrow.

DAY: _____   DAILY THEME: _____

Win the Day Planning

Today, I am grateful I get to be a coach because:

I have reviewed my team, recruiting, administrative & personal goals ☐

Today's Results List: List in priority order the top 3 things you can accomplish that would make a measurable impact on your goals and projects? What metric are you trying to hit? Schedule it.

Priority #1:   **Metric I am aiming for_____**

Priority #2:   **Metric I am aiming for_____**

Priority #3:   **Metric I am aiming for_____**

○ **Morning Routine**   ○ **Workday Startup Routine**

TIME	DAILY SCHEDULE
5 am	
6 am	
7 am	
8 am	
9 am	
10 am	
11 am	
12 pm	
1 pm	
2 pm	
3 pm	
4 pm	
5 pm	
6 pm	
7 pm	
8 pm	
9 pm	
10 pm	
11 pm	

○ **Workday Shutdown Routine**   ○ **Evening Routine**

Person/people I need to Lead or Connect with Today (and How to Do It Well)

What or Who Am I Waiting On To Get a Project Done:

Who Needs Something From Me Today or This Week That I Can Proactively Get To Them?

Staff meeting topics to cover:

Team meeting topics to cover:

21

HOW TO USE PAGE 2 OF THE DAILY EXECUTION PAGE

DAILY LOG

Recruiting, Team, Administration, and Personal Things To-Do. Here is where you will list of all the tasks that you need to carry out for the day. It is important to get your tasks out of your head and put them into a trusted productivity system where you know that you won't forget about them and where you can easily find them when you need them.

1. Organize your To-Do List into categories in an effort to avoid lumping everything you need to do together into one big long list without any order or structure. Batch like tasks together will help you do them more effectively (group emails together, phone calls together, etc.). It's much easier to do related tasks one after another, than interspersing them with un-related tasks.

2. Always prioritize and schedule activities that will lead you in the direction of your vision and goals every single day.

3. Tackle the most important jobs first, and don't waste time on trivial tasks. Do your best to work on low value tasks ONLY AFTER you have gotten some big things done first.

Knowing the top three things that you need to accomplish in a day gives you extra focus and helps you stay on task when you arrive at the office.

PILE UP ZONE

Each Daily Activity page will have an area where you can take note of those random things that interest you throughout the day. These items, more than likely, may not support the goals you are working towards at the time, but these items might be useful later. For example, you might have an idea for a new style or system of play, a new revenue stream through camp, someone you want to collaborate with, etc.? Take note of them here so you can refer back to these gems when you need them.

5 DAILY PILLARS

In order to stay on top of your game, you need to be aware of the daily life sources that fuel you to keep moving forward. Each Daily Activity page has a place where you will take a quick poll of these 5 things: Mental Focus (how focused was your day?), Emotional Energy (anything weighing on you today that is affecting your focus or progress?), Physical Energy (are you moving, did you workout, get your heart rate up?), Life Fuel (did you eat well today, did you skip lunch, how was your sleep?), and Social Connections (did you connect with anyone today that is outside of your direct program?)

WIN TOMORROW TODAY WITH NIGHT BEFORE PLANNING

Basically, now the cycle starts over again. Plan your top 3 priorities the night before or early in the morning. For each activity, ask yourself "Is there a smarter way to achieve the same outcome?

THE DAILY TO-DO'S

Recruiting: 9

Administrative

Time Spent today

Calls/texts to make:

On Campus Visits:

Social Media:

Events to Recruit at:

Time Spent today

Time Spent today

Team:

Personal:

Time Spent today

Time Spent today

PILE UP ZONE: Great ideas, goals, projects, apps or people to follow up on later

10

5 PERFORMANCE PILLARS	Give yourself a score of 1-5. 1=low and 5=high in terms of productivity					What could you do to get 1 point higher?
11 Mental Focus	1	2	3	4	5	
Mental/Emotional/Attitude	1	2	3	4	5	
Productivity	1	2	3	4	5	
Energy	1	2	3	4	5	
Social Connections	1	2	3	4	5	

Win tomorrow today: Plan your top 3 priorities the night before or early in the morning. For each activity, ask yourself "Is there a smarter way to achieve the same outcome?"

12

"Pleasure in the job puts perfection in the work." – Aristotle

MONTH / YEAR:

THEME:

FOCUS AREAS FOR GROWTH AND IMPROVEMENT THIS MONTH	✓
1.	○
2.	○
3.	○

STRATEGIES/PROJECTS TO HELP REACH GOALS

Establish 1-2 projects that are going to help you reach the goals you listed above.

SUNDAY	MONDAY	TUESDAY

Major Events

Write down any major events coming up this month, and how you can prepare for them.

These things MUST happen this month

How do you build your program exponentially in a relatively short amount of time? Through focus. Use this section in each area to drive the direction of your month, week, and day to eliminate activities that just do NOT fit in. Always refer back to your focus and ask yourself..."Am I working on things that support my focus?"

WEDNESDAY	THURSDAY	FRIDAY	SATURDAY

Recruiting deadlines/outcomes we need this month Include:	The best ways I can prepare and ensure that I show up to win this month are:

YOUR IDEAL WEEK

FOCUS AREA FOR GROWTH AND IM-PROVEMENT THIS WEEK	✓
1.	○
2.	○
3.	○

Focus Areas

TIME	MONDAY	TUESDAY	WEDNESDAY
5:00 - 5:30 AM			
6:00 - 6:30 AM			
7:00 - 7:30 AM			
8:00 - 8:30 AM			
9:00 - 9:30 AM			
10:00 - 10:30 AM			
11:00 - 11:30 AM			
12:00 - 12:30 PM			
1:00 - 1:30 PM			
2:00 - 2:30 PM			
3:00 - 3:30 PM			
4:00 - 4:30 PM			
5:00 - 5:30 PM			
6:00 - 6:30 PM			
7:00 - 7:30 PM			
8:00 - 8:30 PM			
9:00 - 9:30 PM			
10:00 - 10:30 PM			
11:00 - 11:30 PM			
12:00 - 12:30 AM			

HOW TO SCHEDULE YOUR IDEAL WEEK

Make time for what matters first.

Note on this calendar when you will have:

1. Family time
2. Weekly reflection
3. Self-care time
4. Wake up time
5. Go to bed time
6. Work stop time
7. Practice
8. Weights
9. Meetings
10. After all of this is set, what big blocks of time to do you have left for the growth and improvement projects you listed above? Find at least 1 hour each day and block it off.
11. Fit all of the busy work in between your blocks of program building projects.

Last week's wins & lessons learned:

USE THIS PAGE TO CREATE AN OVERVIEW FOR NEXT WEEK

THURSDAY	FRIDAY	SATURDAY	SUNDAY

Thoughts for this upcoming week:

DAY: _____   DAILY THEME: _____

	Win the Day Planning

Today, I am grateful I get to be a coach because:

I have reviewed my team, recruiting, administrative & personal goals ☐

Today's Results List: List in priority order the top 3 things you can accomplish that would make a measurable impact on your goals and projects? What metric are you trying to hit? Schedule it.

Priority #1:   Metric I am aiming for_____

Priority #2:   Metric I am aiming for_____

Priority #3:   Metric I am aiming for_____

○ **Morning Routine**   ○ **Workday Startup Routine**

TIME	DAILY SCHEDULE
5 am	
6 am	
7 am	
8 am	
9 am	
10 am	
11 am	
12 pm	
1 pm	
2 pm	
3 pm	
4 pm	
5 pm	
6 pm	
7 pm	
8 pm	
9 pm	
10 pm	
11 pm	

○ **Workday Shutdown Routine**   ○ **Evening Routine**

Person/People I need to Lead or Connect with Today (and How to Do It Well)

Staff meeting topics to cover:

What or Who Am I Waiting On To Get a Project Done:

Team meeting topics to cover:

Who Needs Something From Me Today or This Week That I Can Proactively Get To Them?

THE DAILY TO-DO'S

Recruiting:

Administrative

Calls/texts to make:

Time Spent today

On Campus Visits:

Social Media:

Events to Recruit at:

Time Spent today

Time Spent today

Team:

Personal:

Time Spent today

Time Spent today

PILE UP ZONE: Great ideas, goals, projects, apps or people to follow up on later

5 PERFORMANCE PILLARS	Give yourself a score of 1-5. 1=low and 5=high in terms of productivity					What could you do to get 1 point higher?
Mental Focus	1	2	3	4	5	
Mental/Emotional/Attitude	1	2	3	4	5	
Productivity	1	2	3	4	5	
Energy	1	2	3	4	5	
Social Connections	1	2	3	4	5	

Win tomorrow today: Plan your top 3 priorities the night before or early in the morning. For each activity, ask yourself "Is there a smarter way to achieve the same outcome?"

"Productivity is being able to do things that you were never able to do before." – Franz Kafka

DAY: DAILY THEME:

Win the Day Planning		

Today, I am grateful I get to be a coach because:

I have reviewed my team, recruiting, administrative & personal goals ☐

Today's Results List: List in priority order the top 3 things you can accomplish that would make a measurable impact on your goals and projects? What metric are you trying to hit? Schedule it.

Priority #1:   **Metric I am aiming for_____**

Priority #2:   **Metric I am aiming for_____**

Priority #3:   **Metric I am aiming for_____**

Person/People I need to Lead or Connect with Today (and How to Do It Well)

What or Who Am I Waiting On To Get a Project Done:

Who Needs Something From Me Today or This Week That I Can Proactively Get To Them?

○ **Morning Routine**   ○ **Workday Startup Routine**

TIME	DAILY SCHEDULE
5 am	
6 am	
7 am	
8 am	
9 am	
10 am	
11 am	
12 pm	
1 pm	
2 pm	
3 pm	
4 pm	
5 pm	
6 pm	
7 pm	
8 pm	
9 pm	
10 pm	
11 pm	

○ **Workday Shutdown Routine**   ○ **Evening Routine**

Staff meeting topics to cover:

Team meeting topics to cover:

THE DAILY TO-DO'S

Recruiting:	Administrative
Calls/texts to make:	
	Time Spent today
On Campus Visits:	Social Media:
Events to Recruit at:	
Time Spent today	Time Spent today
Team:	Personal:
Time Spent today	Time Spent today

PILE UP ZONE: Great ideas, goals, projects, apps or people to follow up on later

5 PERFORMANCE PILLARS	Give yourself a score of 1-5. 1=low and 5=high in terms of productivity					What could you do to get 1 point higher?
Mental Focus	1	2	3	4	5	
Mental/Emotional/Attitude	1	2	3	4	5	
Productivity	1	2	3	4	5	
Energy	1	2	3	4	5	
Social Connections	1	2	3	4	5	

Win tomorrow today: Plan your top 3 priorities the night before or early in the morning. For each activity, ask yourself "Is there a smarter way to achieve the same outcome?

"You may delay, but time will not." – Benjamin Franklin

DAY: _____   DAILY THEME: _____

Win the Day Planning

Today, I am grateful I get to be a coach because:

_____

I have reviewed my team, recruiting, administrative & personal goals ☐

Today's Results List: List in priority order the top 3 things you can accomplish that would make a measurable impact on your goals and projects? What metric are you trying to hit? Schedule it.

Priority #1:   Metric I am aiming for_____

Priority #2:   Metric I am aiming for_____

Priority #3:   Metric I am aiming for_____

Person/People I need to Lead or Connect with Today (and How to Do It Well)

What or Who Am I Waiting On To Get a Project Done:

Who Needs Something From Me Today or This Week That I Can Proactively Get To Them?

○ **Morning Routine**   ○ **Workday Startup Routine**

TIME	DAILY SCHEDULE
5 am	
6 am	
7 am	
8 am	
9 am	
10 am	
11 am	
12 pm	
1 pm	
2 pm	
3 pm	
4 pm	
5 pm	
6 pm	
7 pm	
8 pm	
9 pm	
10 pm	
11 pm	

○ **Workday Shutdown Routine**   ○ **Evening Routine**

Staff meeting topics to cover:

Team meeting topics to cover:

THE DAILY TO-DO'S

Recruiting:	Administrative
Calls/texts to make:	
	Time Spent today
On Campus Visits:	Social Media:
Events to Recruit at:	
Time Spent today	Time Spent today
Team:	Personal:
Time Spent today	Time Spent today

PILE UP ZONE: Great ideas, goals, projects, apps or people to follow up on later

5 PERFORMANCE PILLARS	Give yourself a score of 1-5. 1=low and 5=high in terms of productivity					What could you do to get 1 point higher?
Mental Focus	1	2	3	4	5	
Mental/Emotional/Attitude	1	2	3	4	5	
Productivity	1	2	3	4	5	
Energy	1	2	3	4	5	
Social Connections	1	2	3	4	5	

Win tomorrow today: Plan your top 3 priorities the night before or early in the morning.   For each activity, ask yourself "Is there a smarter way to achieve the same outcome?

"The tragedy in life doesn't lie in not reaching your goal. The tragedy lies in having no goal to reach." – Benjamin E. Mays

DAY: _____   DAILY THEME: _____

Win the Day Planning			

Today, I am grateful I get to be a coach because:

I have reviewed my team, recruiting, administrative & personal goals ☐

Today's Results List: List in priority order the top 3 things you can accomplish that would make a measurable impact on your goals and projects? What metric are you trying to hit? Schedule it.

Priority #1:   Metric I am aiming for_____

Priority #2:   Metric I am aiming for_____

Priority #3:   Metric I am aiming for_____

○ **Morning Routine**   ○ **Workday Startup Routine**

TIME	DAILY SCHEDULE
5 am	
6 am	
7 am	
8 am	
9 am	
10 am	
11 am	
12 pm	
1 pm	
2 pm	
3 pm	
4 pm	
5 pm	
6 pm	
7 pm	
8 pm	
9 pm	
10 pm	
11 pm	

○ **Workday Shutdown Routine**   ○ **Evening Routine**

Person/People I need to Lead or Connect with Today (and How to Do It Well)

Staff meeting topics to cover:

What or Who Am I Waiting On To Get a Project Done:

Team meeting topics to cover:

Who Needs Something From Me Today or This Week That I Can Proactively Get To Them?

THE DAILY TO-DO'S

Recruiting:	Administrative
Calls/texts to make:	
	Time Spent today
On Campus Visits:	Social Media:
Events to Recruit at:	
Time Spent today	Time Spent today
Team:	Personal:
Time Spent today	Time Spent today

PILE UP ZONE: Great ideas, goals, projects, apps or people to follow up on later

5 PERFORMANCE PILLARS	Give yourself a score of 1-5, 1=low and 5=high in terms of productivity					What could you do to get 1 point higher?
Mental Focus	1	2	3	4	5	
Mental/Emotional/Attitude	1	2	3	4	5	
Productivity	1	2	3	4	5	
Energy	1	2	3	4	5	
Social Connections	1	2	3	4	5	

Win tomorrow today: Plan your top 3 priorities the night before or early in the morning. For each activity, ask yourself "Is there a smarter way to achieve the same outcome?"

"Both good and bad days should end with productivity. Your mood affairs should never influence your work." – Greg Evans

DAY: DAILY THEME:

Win the Day Planning

Today, I am grateful I get to be a coach because:

I have reviewed my team, recruiting, administrative & personal goals ☐

Today's Results List: List in priority order the top 3 things you can accomplish that would make a measurable impact on your goals and projects? What metric are you trying to hit? Schedule it.

Priority #1:   Metric I am aiming for_____

Priority #2:   Metric I am aiming for_____

Priority #3:   Metric I am aiming for_____

Person/People I need to Lead or Connect with Today (and How to Do It Well)

What or Who Am I Waiting On To Get a Project Done:

Who Needs Something From Me Today or This Week That I Can Proactively Get To Them?

○ **Morning Routine**   ○ **Workday Startup Routine**

TIME	DAILY SCHEDULE
5 am	
6 am	
7 am	
8 am	
9 am	
10 am	
11 am	
12 pm	
1 pm	
2 pm	
3 pm	
4 pm	
5 pm	
6 pm	
7 pm	
8 pm	
9 pm	
10 pm	
11 pm	

○ **Workday Shutdown Routine**   ○ **Evening Routine**

Staff meeting topics to cover:

Team meeting topics to cover:

THE DAILY TO-DO'S

Recruiting:	Administrative
Calls/texts to make:	
	Time Spent today
On Campus Visits:	Social Media:
Events to Recruit at:	
Time Spent today	Time Spent today
Team:	Personal:
Time Spent today	Time Spent today

PILE UP ZONE: Great ideas, goals, projects, apps or people to follow up on later

5 PERFORMANCE PILLARS	Give yourself a score of 1-5. 1=low and 5=high in terms of productivity					What could you do to get 1 point higher?
Mental Focus	1	2	3	4	5	
Mental/Emotional/Attitude	1	2	3	4	5	
Productivity	1	2	3	4	5	
Energy	1	2	3	4	5	
Social Connections	1	2	3	4	5	

Win tomorrow today: Plan your top 3 priorities the night before or early in the morning. For each activity, ask yourself "Is there a smarter way to achieve the same outcome?

"Focus on being productive instead of busy." -Tim Ferriss

DAY: DAILY THEME:

Win the Day Planning

Today, I am grateful I get to be a coach because:

I have reviewed my team, recruiting, administrative & personal goals ☐

Today's Results List: List in priority order the top 3 things you can accomplish that would make a measurable impact on your goals and projects? What metric are you trying to hit? Schedule it.

Priority #1:   Metric I am aiming for_____

Priority #2:   Metric I am aiming for_____

Priority #3:   Metric I am aiming for_____

Person/People I need to Lead or Connect with Today (and How to Do It Well)

What or Who Am I Waiting On To Get a Project Done:

Who Needs Something From Me Today or This Week That I Can Proactively Get To Them?

○ **Morning Routine**   ○ **Workday Startup Routine**

TIME	DAILY SCHEDULE
5 am	
6 am	
7 am	
8 am	
9 am	
10 am	
11 am	
12 pm	
1 pm	
2 pm	
3 pm	
4 pm	
5 pm	
6 pm	
7 pm	
8 pm	
9 pm	
10 pm	
11 pm	

○ **Workday Shutdown Routine**   ○ **Evening Routine**

Staff meeting topics to cover:

Team meeting topics to cover:

THE DAILY TO-DO'S

Recruiting:

Calls/texts to make:

On Campus Visits:

Events to Recruit at:

Time Spent today

Team:

Time Spent today

Administrative

Time Spent today

Social Media:

Time Spent today

Personal:

Time Spent today

PILE UP ZONE: Great ideas, goals, projects, apps or people to follow up on later

5 PERFORMANCE PILLARS	Give yourself a score of 1-5, 1=low and 5=high in terms of productivity					What could you do to get 1 point higher?
Mental Focus	1	2	3	4	5	
Mental/Emotional/Attitude	1	2	3	4	5	
Productivity	1	2	3	4	5	
Energy	1	2	3	4	5	
Social Connections	1	2	3	4	5	

Win tomorrow today: Plan your top 3 priorities the night before or early in the morning. For each activity, ask yourself "Is there a smarter way to achieve the same outcome?

"Productivity is never an accident. It is always the result of a commitment to excellence, intelligent planning, and focused effort." – Paul J. Meyer

DAY: DAILY THEME:

Win the Day Planning

Today, I am grateful I get to be a coach because:

I have reviewed my team, recruiting, administrative & personal goals ☐

Today's Results List: List in priority order the top 3 things you can accomplish that would make a measurable impact on your goals and projects? What metric are you trying to hit? Schedule it.

Priority #1:   **Metric I am aiming for_____**

Priority #2:   **Metric I am aiming for_____**

Priority #3:   **Metric I am aiming for_____**

Person/People I need to Lead or Connect with Today (and How to Do It Well)

What or Who Am I Waiting On To Get a Project Done:

Who Needs Something From Me Today or This Week That I Can Proactively Get To Them?

○ **Morning Routine**   ○ **Workday Startup Routine**

TIME	DAILY SCHEDULE
5 am	
6 am	
7 am	
8 am	
9 am	
10 am	
11 am	
12 pm	
1 pm	
2 pm	
3 pm	
4 pm	
5 pm	
6 pm	
7 pm	
8 pm	
9 pm	
10 pm	
11 pm	

○ **Workday Shutdown Routine**   ○ **Evening Routine**

Staff meeting topics to cover:

Team meeting topics to cover:

THE DAILY TO-DO'S

Recruiting:	Administrative
Calls/texts to make:	
	Time Spent today
On Campus Visits:	Social Media:
Events to Recruit at:	
	Time Spent today
Time Spent today	
Team:	Personal:
Time Spent today	Time Spent today

PILE UP ZONE: Great ideas, goals, projects, apps or people to follow up on later

5 PERFORMANCE PILLARS	Give yourself a score of 1-5, 1=low and 5=high in terms of productivity					What could you do to get 1 point higher?
Mental Focus	1	2	3	4	5	
Mental/Emotional/Attitude	1	2	3	4	5	
Productivity	1	2	3	4	5	
Energy	1	2	3	4	5	
Social Connections	1	2	3	4	5	

Win tomorrow today: Plan your top 3 priorities the night before or early in the morning. For each activity, ask yourself "Is there a smarter way to achieve the same outcome?

"Until we can manage time, we can manage nothing else." – Peter Drucker

DAY: _____   DAILY THEME: _____

Win the Day Planning	⭘ **Morning Routine** ⭘ **Workday Startup Routine**

Today, I am grateful I get to be a coach because:

I have reviewed my team, recruiting, administrative & personal goals ☐

Today's Results List: List in priority order the top 3 things you can accomplish that would make a measurable impact on your goals and projects? What metric are you trying to hit? Schedule it.

Priority #1:   Metric I am aiming for_____

Priority #2:   Metric I am aiming for_____

Priority #3:   Metric I am aiming for_____

TIME	DAILY SCHEDULE
5 am	
6 am	
7 am	
8 am	
9 am	
10 am	
11 am	
12 pm	
1 pm	
2 pm	
3 pm	
4 pm	
5 pm	
6 pm	
7 pm	
8 pm	
9 pm	
10 pm	
11 pm	

⭘ **Workday Shutdown Routine**   ⭘ **Evening Routine**

Person/People I need to Lead or Connect with Today (and How to Do It Well)

Staff meeting topics to cover:

What or Who Am I Waiting On To Get a Project Done:

Team meeting topics to cover:

Who Needs Something From Me Today or This Week That I Can Proactively Get To Them?

THE DAILY TO-DO'S

Recruiting:

Administrative

Calls/texts to make:

Time Spent today

On Campus Visits:

Social Media:

Events to Recruit at:

Time Spent today

Time Spent today

Team:

Personal:

Time Spent today

Time Spent today

PILE UP ZONE: Great ideas, goals, projects, apps or people to follow up on later

5 PERFORMANCE PILLARS	Give yourself a score of 1-5, 1=low and 5=high in terms of productivity					What could you do to get 1 point higher?
Mental Focus	1	2	3	4	5	
Mental/Emotional/Attitude	1	2	3	4	5	
Productivity	1	2	3	4	5	
Energy	1	2	3	4	5	
Social Connections	1	2	3	4	5	

Win tomorrow today: Plan your top 3 priorities the night before or early in the morning. For each activity, ask yourself "Is there a smarter way to achieve the same outcome?

"Time is not refundable; use it with intention." – Unknown

DAY: _____   DAILY THEME: _____

Win the Day Planning

Today, I am grateful I get to be a coach because:

I have reviewed my team, recruiting, administrative & personal goals ☐

Today's Results List: List in priority order the top 3 things you can accomplish that would make a measurable impact on your goals and projects? What metric are you trying to hit? Schedule it.

Priority #1:   Metric I am aiming for_____

Priority #2:   Metric I am aiming for_____

Priority #3:   Metric I am aiming for_____

Person/People I need to Lead or Connect with Today (and How to Do It Well)

What or Who Am I Waiting On To Get a Project Done:

Who Needs Something From Me Today or This Week That I Can Proactively Get To Them?

○ **Morning Routine**   ○ **Workday Startup Routine**

TIME	DAILY SCHEDULE
5 am	
6 am	
7 am	
8 am	
9 am	
10 am	
11 am	
12 pm	
1 pm	
2 pm	
3 pm	
4 pm	
5 pm	
6 pm	
7 pm	
8 pm	
9 pm	
10 pm	
11 pm	

○ **Workday Shutdown Routine**   ○ **Evening Routine**

Staff meeting topics to cover:

Team meeting topics to cover:

THE DAILY TO-DO'S

Recruiting:

Calls/texts to make:

On Campus Visits:

Events to Recruit at:

| Time Spent today |

Team:

| Time Spent today |

Administrative

| Time Spent today |

Social Media:

| Time Spent today |

Personal:

| Time Spent today |

PILE UP ZONE: Great ideas, goals, projects, apps or people to follow up on later

5 PERFORMANCE PILLARS	Give yourself a score of 1-5, 1=low and 5=high in terms of productivity					What could you do to get 1 point higher?
Mental Focus	1	2	3	4	5	
Mental/Emotional/Attitude	1	2	3	4	5	
Productivity	1	2	3	4	5	
Energy	1	2	3	4	5	
Social Connections	1	2	3	4	5	

Win tomorrow today: Plan your top 3 priorities the night before or early in the morning. For each activity, ask yourself "Is there a smarter way to achieve the same outcome?

"You don't get paid for the hour, you get paid for the value you bring to the hour." – Jim Rohn

45

DAY: DAILY THEME:

Win the Day Planning		

Today, I am grateful I get to be a coach because:

I have reviewed my team, recruiting, administrative & personal goals ☐

Today's Results List: List in priority order the top 3 things you can accomplish that would make a measurable impact on your goals and projects? What metric are you trying to hit? Schedule it.

Priority #1:   Metric I am aiming for_____

Priority #2:   Metric I am aiming for_____

Priority #3:   Metric I am aiming for_____

Person/People I need to Lead or Connect with Today (and How to Do It Well)

What or Who Am I Waiting On To Get a Project Done:

Who Needs Something From Me Today or This Week That I Can Proactively Get To Them?

○ **Morning Routine**   ○ **Workday Startup Routine**

TIME	DAILY SCHEDULE
5 am	
6 am	
7 am	
8 am	
9 am	
10 am	
11 am	
12 pm	
1 pm	
2 pm	
3 pm	
4 pm	
5 pm	
6 pm	
7 pm	
8 pm	
9 pm	
10 pm	
11 pm	

○ **Workday Shutdown Routine**   ○ **Evening Routine**

Staff meeting topics to cover:

Team meeting topics to cover:

THE DAILY TO-DO'S

Recruiting:

Administrative

Calls/texts to make:

Time Spent today

On Campus Visits:

Social Media:

Events to Recruit at:

Time Spent today

Time Spent today

Team:

Personal:

Time Spent today

Time Spent today

PILE UP ZONE: Great ideas, goals, projects, apps or people to follow up on later

5 PERFORMANCE PILLARS	Give yourself a score of 1-5. 1=low and 5=high in terms of productivity					What could you do to get 1 point higher?
Mental Focus	1	2	3	4	5	
Mental/Emotional/Attitude	1	2	3	4	5	
Productivity	1	2	3	4	5	
Energy	1	2	3	4	5	
Social Connections	1	2	3	4	5	

Win tomorrow today: Plan your top 3 priorities the night before or early in the morning. For each activity, ask yourself "Is there a smarter way to achieve the same outcome?"

"Don't confuse activity with productivity. Many people are simply busy being busy." – Robin Sharma

DAY: DAILY THEME:

Win the Day Planning

Today, I am grateful I get to be a coach because:

I have reviewed my team, recruiting, administrative & personal goals ☐

Today's Results List: List in priority order the top 3 things you can accomplish that would make a measurable impact on your goals and projects? What metric are you trying to hit? Schedule it.

Priority #1:   **Metric I am aiming for_____**

Priority #2:   **Metric I am aiming for_____**

Priority #3:   **Metric I am aiming for_____**

Person/People I need to Lead or Connect with Today (and How to Do It Well)

What or Who Am I Waiting On To Get a Project Done:

Who Needs Something From Me Today or This Week That I Can Proactively Get To Them?

○ **Morning Routine**   ○ **Workday Startup Routine**

TIME	DAILY SCHEDULE
5 am	
6 am	
7 am	
8 am	
9 am	
10 am	
11 am	
12 pm	
1 pm	
2 pm	
3 pm	
4 pm	
5 pm	
6 pm	
7 pm	
8 pm	
9 pm	
10 pm	
11 pm	

○ **Workday Shutdown Routine**   ○ **Evening Routine**

Staff meeting topics to cover:

Team meeting topics to cover:

THE DAILY TO-DO'S

Recruiting:

Administrative

Calls/texts to make:

Time Spent today

On Campus Visits:

Social Media:

Events to Recruit at:

Time Spent today

Time Spent today

Team:

Personal:

Time Spent today

Time Spent today

PILE UP ZONE: Great ideas, goals, projects, apps or people to follow up on later

5 PERFORMANCE PILLARS	Give yourself a score of 1-5, 1=low and 5=high in terms of productivity					What could you do to get 1 point higher?
Mental Focus	1	2	3	4	5	
Mental/Emotional/Attitude	1	2	3	4	5	
Productivity	1	2	3	4	5	
Energy	1	2	3	4	5	
Social Connections	1	2	3	4	5	

Win tomorrow today: Plan your top 3 priorities the night before or early in the morning. For each activity, ask yourself "Is there a smarter way to achieve the same outcome?"

"If we all did the things we are capable of doing, we would literally astound ourselves." – Thomas Edison

DAY: DAILY THEME:

Win the Day Planning

Today, I am grateful I get to be a coach because:

I have reviewed my team, recruiting, administrative & personal goals ☐

Today's Results List: List in priority order the top 3 things you can accomplish that would make a measurable impact on your goals and projects? What metric are you trying to hit? Schedule it.

Priority #1:   Metric I am aiming for_____

Priority #2:   Metric I am aiming for_____

Priority #3:   Metric I am aiming for_____

Person/People I need to Lead or Connect with Today (and How to Do It Well)

What or Who Am I Waiting On To Get a Project Done:

Who Needs Something From Me Today or This Week That I Can Proactively Get To Them?

○ **Morning Routine**   ○ **Workday Startup Routine**

TIME	DAILY SCHEDULE
5 am	
6 am	
7 am	
8 am	
9 am	
10 am	
11 am	
12 pm	
1 pm	
2 pm	
3 pm	
4 pm	
5 pm	
6 pm	
7 pm	
8 pm	
9 pm	
10 pm	
11 pm	

○ **Workday Shutdown Routine**   ○ **Evening Routine**

Staff meeting topics to cover:

Team meeting topics to cover:

THE DAILY TO-DO'S

Recruiting:

Calls/texts to make:

On Campus Visits:

Events to Recruit at:

Time Spent today

Administrative

Time Spent today

Social Media:

Time Spent today

Team:

Time Spent today

Personal:

Time Spent today

PILE UP ZONE: Great ideas, goals, projects, apps or people to follow up on later

5 PERFORMANCE PILLARS	Give yourself a score of 1-5, 1=low and 5=high in terms of productivity					What could you do to get 1 point higher?
Mental Focus	1	2	3	4	5	
Mental/Emotional/Attitude	1	2	3	4	5	
Productivity	1	2	3	4	5	
Energy	1	2	3	4	5	
Social Connections	1	2	3	4	5	

Win tomorrow today: Plan your top 3 priorities the night before or early in the morning. For each activity, ask yourself "Is there a smarter way to achieve the same outcome?"

"There is never enough time to do it right, but there is always enough time to do it over." – John W. Bergman

DAY: DAILY THEME:

Win the Day Planning

Today, I am grateful I get to be a coach because:

I have reviewed my team, recruiting, administrative & personal goals ☐

Today's Results List: List in priority order the top 3 things you can accomplish that would make a measurable impact on your goals and projects? What metric are you trying to hit? Schedule it.

Priority #1:   **Metric I am aiming for_____**

Priority #2:   **Metric I am aiming for_____**

Priority #3:   **Metric I am aiming for_____**

○ **Morning Routine**   ○ **Workday Startup Routine**

TIME	DAILY SCHEDULE
5 am	
6 am	
7 am	
8 am	
9 am	
10 am	
11 am	
12 pm	
1 pm	
2 pm	
3 pm	
4 pm	
5 pm	
6 pm	
7 pm	
8 pm	
9 pm	
10 pm	
11 pm	

○ **Workday Shutdown Routine**   ○ **Evening Routine**

Person/People I need to Lead or Connect with Today (and How to Do It Well)

Staff meeting topics to cover:

What or Who Am I Waiting On To Get a Project Done:

Team meeting topics to cover:

Who Needs Something From Me Today or This Week That I Can Proactively Get To Them?

THE DAILY TO-DO'S

Recruiting:

Administrative

Calls/texts to make:

Time Spent today

On Campus Visits:

Social Media:

Events to Recruit at:

Time Spent today

Time Spent today

Team:

Personal:

Time Spent today

Time Spent today

PILE UP ZONE: Great ideas, goals, projects, apps or people to follow up on later

5 PERFORMANCE PILLARS	Give yourself a score of 1-5. 1=low and 5=high in terms of productivity					What could you do to get 1 point higher?
Mental Focus	1	2	3	4	5	
Mental/Emotional/Attitude	1	2	3	4	5	
Productivity	1	2	3	4	5	
Energy	1	2	3	4	5	
Social Connections	1	2	3	4	5	

Win tomorrow today: Plan your top 3 priorities the night before or early in the morning. For each activity, ask yourself "Is there a smarter way to achieve the same outcome?"

"The way to get started is to quit talking and begin doing." – Walt Disney

DAY: DAILY THEME:

Win the Day Planning	

Today, I am grateful I get to be a coach because:

I have reviewed my team, recruiting, administrative & personal goals ☐

Today's Results List: List in priority order the top 3 things you can accomplish that would make a measurable impact on your goals and projects? What metric are you trying to hit? Schedule it.

Priority #1:   Metric I am aiming for_____

Priority #2:   Metric I am aiming for_____

Priority #3:   Metric I am aiming for_____

Person/People I need to Lead or Connect with Today (and How to Do It Well)

What or Who Am I Waiting On To Get a Project Done:

Who Needs Something From Me Today or This Week That I Can Proactively Get To Them?

○ **Morning Routine**   ○ **Workday Startup Routine**

TIME	DAILY SCHEDULE
5 am	
6 am	
7 am	
8 am	
9 am	
10 am	
11 am	
12 pm	
1 pm	
2 pm	
3 pm	
4 pm	
5 pm	
6 pm	
7 pm	
8 pm	
9 pm	
10 pm	
11 pm	

○ **Workday Shutdown Routine**   ○ **Evening Routine**

Staff meeting topics to cover:

Team meeting topics to cover:

THE DAILY TO-DO'S

Recruiting:

Administrative

Calls/texts to make:

Time Spent today

On Campus Visits:

Social Media:

Events to Recruit at:

Time Spent today

Time Spent today

Team:

Personal:

Time Spent today

Time Spent today

PILE UP ZONE: Great ideas, goals, projects, apps or people to follow up on later

5 PERFORMANCE PILLARS	Give yourself a score of 1-5, 1=low and 5=high in terms of productivity					What could you do to get 1 point higher?
Mental Focus	1	2	3	4	5	
Mental/Emotional/Attitude	1	2	3	4	5	
Productivity	1	2	3	4	5	
Energy	1	2	3	4	5	
Social Connections	1	2	3	4	5	

Win tomorrow today: Plan your top 3 priorities the night before or early in the morning. For each activity, ask yourself "Is there a smarter way to achieve the same outcome?"

"You don't need a new plan for next year. You need a commitment." – Seth Godin

DAY: DAILY THEME:

Win the Day Planning

Today, I am grateful I get to be a coach because:

I have reviewed my team, recruiting, administrative & personal goals ☐

Today's Results List: List in priority order the top 3 things you can accomplish that would make a measurable impact on your goals and projects? What metric are you trying to hit? Schedule it.

Priority #1:   Metric I am aiming for_____

Priority #2:   Metric I am aiming for_____

Priority #3:   Metric I am aiming for_____

Person/People I need to Lead or Connect with Today (and How to Do It Well)

What or Who Am I Waiting On To Get a Project Done:

Who Needs Something From Me Today or This Week That I Can Proactively Get To Them?

○ **Morning Routine**   ○ **Workday Startup Routine**

TIME	DAILY SCHEDULE
5 am	
6 am	
7 am	
8 am	
9 am	
10 am	
11 am	
12 pm	
1 pm	
2 pm	
3 pm	
4 pm	
5 pm	
6 pm	
7 pm	
8 pm	
9 pm	
10 pm	
11 pm	

○ **Workday Shutdown Routine**   ○ **Evening Routine**

Staff meeting topics to cover:

Team meeting topics to cover:

THE DAILY TO-DO'S

Recruiting:	Administrative
Calls/texts to make:	
	Time Spent today
On Campus Visits:	Social Media:
Events to Recruit at:	
Time Spent today	Time Spent today
Team:	Personal:
Time Spent today	Time Spent today

PILE UP ZONE: Great ideas, goals, projects, apps or people to follow up on later

5 PERFORMANCE PILLARS	Give yourself a score of 1-5, 1=low and 5=high in terms of productivity					What could you do to get 1 point higher?
Mental Focus	1	2	3	4	5	
Mental/Emotional/Attitude	1	2	3	4	5	
Productivity	1	2	3	4	5	
Energy	1	2	3	4	5	
Social Connections	1	2	3	4	5	

Win tomorrow today: Plan your top 3 priorities the night before or early in the morning. For each activity, ask yourself "Is there a smarter way to achieve the same outcome?"

"Efficiency is doing things right. Effectiveness is doing the right things." – Peter Drucker

DAY: DAILY THEME:

Win the Day Planning

Today, I am grateful I get to be a coach because:

I have reviewed my team, recruiting, administrative & personal goals ☐

Today's Results List: List in priority order the top 3 things you can accomplish that would make a measurable impact on your goals and projects? What metric are you trying to hit? Schedule it.

Priority #1:   **Metric I am aiming for_____**

Priority #2:   **Metric I am aiming for_____**

Priority #3:   **Metric I am aiming for_____**

Person/People I need to Lead or Connect with Today (and How to Do It Well)

What or Who Am I Waiting On To Get a Project Done:

Who Needs Something From Me Today or This Week That I Can Proactively Get To Them?

○ **Morning Routine**   ○ **Workday Startup Routine**

TIME	DAILY SCHEDULE
5 am	
6 am	
7 am	
8 am	
9 am	
10 am	
11 am	
12 pm	
1 pm	
2 pm	
3 pm	
4 pm	
5 pm	
6 pm	
7 pm	
8 pm	
9 pm	
10 pm	
11 pm	

○ **Workday Shutdown Routine**   ○ **Evening Routine**

Staff meeting topics to cover:

Team meeting topics to cover:

THE DAILY TO-DO'S

Recruiting:	Administrative
Calls/texts to make:	
	Time Spent today
On Campus Visits:	Social Media:
Events to Recruit at:	
Time Spent today	Time Spent today
Team:	Personal:
Time Spent today	Time Spent today

PILE UP ZONE: Great ideas, goals, projects, apps or people to follow up on later

5 PERFORMANCE PILLARS	Give yourself a score of 1-5, 1=low and 5=high in terms of productivity					What could you do to get 1 point higher?
Mental Focus	1	2	3	4	5	
Mental/Emotional/Attitude	1	2	3	4	5	
Productivity	1	2	3	4	5	
Energy	1	2	3	4	5	
Social Connections	1	2	3	4	5	

Win tomorrow today: Plan your top 3 priorities the night before or early in the morning. For each activity, ask yourself "Is there a smarter way to achieve the same outcome?

"Working on the right thing is probably more important than working hard." – Caterina Fake

DAY: DAILY THEME:

Win the Day Planning

Today, I am grateful I get to be a coach because:

I have reviewed my team, recruiting, administrative & personal goals ☐

Today's Results List: List in priority order the top 3 things you can accomplish that would make a measurable impact on your goals and projects? What metric are you trying to hit? Schedule it.

Priority #1:   **Metric I am aiming for_____**

Priority #2:   **Metric I am aiming for_____**

Priority #3:   **Metric I am aiming for_____**

Person/People I need to Lead or Connect with Today (and How to Do It Well)

What or Who Am I Waiting On To Get a Project Done:

Who Needs Something From Me Today or This Week That I Can Proactively Get To Them?

○ **Morning Routine**   ○ **Workday Startup Routine**

TIME	DAILY SCHEDULE
5 am	
6 am	
7 am	
8 am	
9 am	
10 am	
11 am	
12 pm	
1 pm	
2 pm	
3 pm	
4 pm	
5 pm	
6 pm	
7 pm	
8 pm	
9 pm	
10 pm	
11 pm	

○ **Workday Shutdown Routine**   ○ **Evening Routine**

Staff meeting topics to cover:

Team meeting topics to cover:

THE DAILY TO-DO'S

Recruiting:

Administrative

Calls/texts to make:

Time Spent today

On Campus Visits:

Social Media:

Events to Recruit at:

Time Spent today

Time Spent today

Team:

Personal:

Time Spent today

Time Spent today

PILE UP ZONE: Great ideas, goals, projects, apps or people to follow up on later

5 PERFORMANCE PILLARS	Give yourself a score of 1-5. 1=low and 5=high in terms of productivity					What could you do to get 1 point higher?
Mental Focus	1	2	3	4	5	
Mental/Emotional/Attitude	1	2	3	4	5	
Productivity	1	2	3	4	5	
Energy	1	2	3	4	5	
Social Connections	1	2	3	4	5	

Win tomorrow today: Plan your top 3 priorities the night before or early in the morning. For each activity, ask yourself "Is there a smarter way to achieve the same outcome?"

"There is no substitute for hard work." – Thomas Edison

DAY: DAILY THEME:

Win the Day Planning

Today, I am grateful I get to be a coach because:

I have reviewed my team, recruiting, administrative & personal goals ☐

Today's Results List: List in priority order the top 3 things you can accomplish that would make a measurable impact on your goals and projects? What metric are you trying to hit? Schedule it.

Priority #1:   Metric I am aiming for_____

Priority #2:   Metric I am aiming for_____

Priority #3:   Metric I am aiming for_____

○ **Morning Routine**   ○ **Workday Startup Routine**

TIME	DAILY SCHEDULE
5 am	
6 am	
7 am	
8 am	
9 am	
10 am	
11 am	
12 pm	
1 pm	
2 pm	
3 pm	
4 pm	
5 pm	
6 pm	
7 pm	
8 pm	
9 pm	
10 pm	
11 pm	

○ **Workday Shutdown Routine**   ○ **Evening Routine**

Staff meeting topics to cover:

Person/People I need to Lead or Connect with Today (and How to Do It Well)

What or Who Am I Waiting On To Get a Project Done:

Team meeting topics to cover:

Who Needs Something From Me Today or This Week That I Can Proactively Get To Them?

THE DAILY TO-DO'S

Recruiting:

Administrative

Calls/texts to make:

Time Spent today

On Campus Visits:

Social Media:

Events to Recruit at:

Time Spent today

Time Spent today

Team:

Personal:

Time Spent today

Time Spent today

PILE UP ZONE: Great ideas, goals, projects, apps or people to follow up on later

5 PERFORMANCE PILLARS	Give yourself a score of 1-5, 1=low and 5=high in terms of productivity					What could you do to get 1 point higher?
Mental Focus	1	2	3	4	5	
Mental/Emotional/Attitude	1	2	3	4	5	
Productivity	1	2	3	4	5	
Energy	1	2	3	4	5	
Social Connections	1	2	3	4	5	

Win tomorrow today: Plan your top 3 priorities the night before or early in the morning. For each activity, ask yourself "Is there a smarter way to achieve the same outcome?"

"The key to productivity is to rotate your avoidance techniques." – Shannon Wheeler

DAY: DAILY THEME:

Win the Day Planning

Today, I am grateful I get to be a coach because:

I have reviewed my team, recruiting, administrative & personal goals ☐

Today's Results List: List in priority order the top 3 things you can accomplish that would make a measurable impact on your goals and projects? What metric are you trying to hit? Schedule it.

Priority #1:   **Metric I am aiming for_____**

Priority #2:   **Metric I am aiming for_____**

Priority #3:   **Metric I am aiming for_____**

Person/People I need to Lead or Connect with Today (and How to Do It Well)

What or Who Am I Waiting On To Get a Project Done:

Who Needs Something From Me Today or This Week That I Can Proactively Get To Them?

○ **Morning Routine**   ○ **Workday Startup Routine**

TIME	DAILY SCHEDULE
5 am	
6 am	
7 am	
8 am	
9 am	
10 am	
11 am	
12 pm	
1 pm	
2 pm	
3 pm	
4 pm	
5 pm	
6 pm	
7 pm	
8 pm	
9 pm	
10 pm	
11 pm	

○ **Workday Shutdown Routine**   ○ **Evening Routine**

Staff meeting topics to cover:

Team meeting topics to cover:

THE DAILY TO-DO'S

Recruiting:	Administrative
Calls/texts to make:	
	Time Spent today
On Campus Visits:	Social Media:
Events to Recruit at:	
Time Spent today	Time Spent today
Team:	Personal:
Time Spent today	Time Spent today

PILE UP ZONE: Great ideas, goals, projects, apps or people to follow up on later

5 PERFORMANCE PILLARS	Give yourself a score of 1-5, 1=low and 5=high in terms of productivity					What could you do to get 1 point higher?
Mental Focus	1	2	3	4	5	
Mental/Emotional/Attitude	1	2	3	4	5	
Productivity	1	2	3	4	5	
Energy	1	2	3	4	5	
Social Connections	1	2	3	4	5	

Win tomorrow today: Plan your top 3 priorities the night before or early in the morning. For each activity, ask yourself "Is there a smarter way to achieve the same outcome?"

"Create with the heart; build with the mind." – Criss Jami

DAY: _____   DAILY THEME: _____

Win the Day Planning

Today, I am grateful I get to be a coach because:

I have reviewed my team, recruiting, administrative & personal goals ☐

Today's Results List: List in priority order the top 3 things you can accomplish that would make a measurable impact on your goals and projects? What metric are you trying to hit? Schedule it.

Priority #1:   Metric I am aiming for_____

Priority #2:   Metric I am aiming for_____

Priority #3:   Metric I am aiming for_____

○ **Morning Routine**   ○ **Workday Startup Routine**

TIME	DAILY SCHEDULE
5 am	
6 am	
7 am	
8 am	
9 am	
10 am	
11 am	
12 pm	
1 pm	
2 pm	
3 pm	
4 pm	
5 pm	
6 pm	
7 pm	
8 pm	
9 pm	
10 pm	
11 pm	

○ **Workday Shutdown Routine**   ○ **Evening Routine**

Person/People I need to Lead or Connect with Today (and How to Do It Well)

Staff meeting topics to cover:

What or Who Am I Waiting On To Get a Project Done:

Team meeting topics to cover:

Who Needs Something From Me Today or This Week That I Can Proactively Get To Them?

THE DAILY TO-DO'S

Recruiting:	Administrative
Calls/texts to make:	
	Time Spent today
On Campus Visits:	Social Media:
Events to Recruit at:	
Time Spent today	Time Spent today
Team:	Personal:
Time Spent today	Time Spent today

PILE UP ZONE: Great ideas, goals, projects, apps or people to follow up on later

5 PERFORMANCE PILLARS	Give yourself a score of 1-5, 1=low and 5=high in terms of productivity					What could you do to get 1 point higher?
Mental Focus	1	2	3	4	5	
Mental/Emotional/Attitude	1	2	3	4	5	
Productivity	1	2	3	4	5	
Energy	1	2	3	4	5	
Social Connections	1	2	3	4	5	

Win tomorrow today: Plan your top 3 priorities the night before or early in the morning. For each activity, ask yourself "Is there a smarter way to achieve the same outcome?"

"Life is too complicated not to be orderly."– Martha Stewart

DAY: DAILY THEME:

Win the Day Planning	○ **Morning Routine** ○ **Workday Startup Routine**

Today, I am grateful I get to be a coach because:

I have reviewed my team, recruiting, administrative & personal goals ☐

Today's Results List: List in priority order the top 3 things you can accomplish that would make a measurable impact on your goals and projects? What metric are you trying to hit? Schedule it.

Priority #1:   **Metric I am aiming for_____**

Priority #2:   **Metric I am aiming for_____**

Priority #3:   **Metric I am aiming for_____**

TIME	DAILY SCHEDULE
5 am	
6 am	
7 am	
8 am	
9 am	
10 am	
11 am	
12 pm	
1 pm	
2 pm	
3 pm	
4 pm	
5 pm	
6 pm	
7 pm	
8 pm	
9 pm	
10 pm	
11 pm	

○ **Workday Shutdown Routine**   ○ **Evening Routine**

Person/People I need to Lead or Connect with Today (and How to Do It Well)

Staff meeting topics to cover:

What or Who Am I Waiting On To Get a Project Done:

Team meeting topics to cover:

Who Needs Something From Me Today or This Week That I Can Proactively Get To Them?

THE DAILY TO-DO'S

Recruiting:

Administrative

Calls/texts to make:

Time Spent today

On Campus Visits:

Social Media:

Events to Recruit at:

Time Spent today

Time Spent today

Team:

Personal:

Time Spent today

Time Spent today

PILE UP ZONE: Great ideas, goals, projects, apps or people to follow up on later

5 PERFORMANCE PILLARS	Give yourself a score of 1-5, 1=low and 5=high in terms of productivity					What could you do to get 1 point higher?
Mental Focus	1	2	3	4	5	
Mental/Emotional/Attitude	1	2	3	4	5	
Productivity	1	2	3	4	5	
Energy	1	2	3	4	5	
Social Connections	1	2	3	4	5	

Win tomorrow today: Plan your top 3 priorities the night before or early in the morning. For each activity, ask yourself "Is there a smarter way to achieve the same outcome?

"Make each day your masterpiece."– John Wooden

DAY: DAILY THEME:

Win the Day Planning

Today, I am grateful I get to be a coach because:

I have reviewed my team, recruiting, administrative & personal goals ☐

Today's Results List: List in priority order the top 3 things you can accomplish that would make a measurable impact on your goals and projects? What metric are you trying to hit? Schedule it.

Priority #1:   Metric I am aiming for_____

Priority #2:   Metric I am aiming for_____

Priority #3:   Metric I am aiming for_____

○ **Morning Routine**   ○ **Workday Startup Routine**

TIME	DAILY SCHEDULE
5 am	
6 am	
7 am	
8 am	
9 am	
10 am	
11 am	
12 pm	
1 pm	
2 pm	
3 pm	
4 pm	
5 pm	
6 pm	
7 pm	
8 pm	
9 pm	
10 pm	
11 pm	

○ **Workday Shutdown Routine**   ○ **Evening Routine**

Person/People I need to Lead or Connect with Today (and How to Do It Well)

Staff meeting topics to cover:

What or Who Am I Waiting On To Get a Project Done:

Team meeting topics to cover:

Who Needs Something From Me Today or This Week That I Can Proactively Get To Them?

THE DAILY TO-DO'S

Recruiting:

Calls/texts to make:

On Campus Visits:

Events to Recruit at:

Time Spent today

Team:

Time Spent today

Administrative

Time Spent today

Social Media:

Time Spent today

Personal:

Time Spent today

PILE UP ZONE: Great ideas, goals, projects, apps or people to follow up on later

5 PERFORMANCE PILLARS	Give yourself a score of 1-5, 1=low and 5=high in terms of productivity					What could you do to get 1 point higher?
Mental Focus	1	2	3	4	5	
Mental/Emotional/Attitude	1	2	3	4	5	
Productivity	1	2	3	4	5	
Energy	1	2	3	4	5	
Social Connections	1	2	3	4	5	

Win tomorrow today: Plan your top 3 priorities the night before or early in the morning. For each activity, ask yourself "Is there a smarter way to achieve the same outcome?

"Position yourself to succeed by doing the other things in your life that rejuvenate you. Exhaustion affects your quality and productivity."– Jeff VanderMeer

DAY: DAILY THEME:

Win the Day Planning

Today, I am grateful I get to be a coach because:

I have reviewed my team, recruiting, administrative & personal goals ☐

Today's Results List: List in priority order the top 3 things you can accomplish that would make a measurable impact on your goals and projects? What metric are you trying to hit? Schedule it.

Priority #1:   Metric I am aiming for_____

Priority #2:   Metric I am aiming for_____

Priority #3:   Metric I am aiming for_____

○ **Morning Routine**   ○ **Workday Startup Routine**

TIME	DAILY SCHEDULE
5 am	
6 am	
7 am	
8 am	
9 am	
10 am	
11 am	
12 pm	
1 pm	
2 pm	
3 pm	
4 pm	
5 pm	
6 pm	
7 pm	
8 pm	
9 pm	
10 pm	
11 pm	

○ **Workday Shutdown Routine**   ○ **Evening Routine**

Person/People I need to Lead or Connect with Today (and How to Do It Well)

Staff meeting topics to cover:

What or Who Am I Waiting On To Get a Project Done:

Team meeting topics to cover:

Who Needs Something From Me Today or This Week That I Can Proactively Get To Them?

THE DAILY TO-DO'S

Recruiting:

Calls/texts to make:

On Campus Visits:

Events to Recruit at:

Time Spent today

Administrative

Time Spent today

Social Media:

Time Spent today

Team:

Time Spent today

Personal:

Time Spent today

PILE UP ZONE: Great ideas, goals, projects, apps or people to follow up on later

5 PERFORMANCE PILLARS	Give yourself a score of 1-5, 1=low and 5=high in terms of productivity					What could you do to get 1 point higher?
Mental Focus	1	2	3	4	5	
Mental/Emotional/Attitude	1	2	3	4	5	
Productivity	1	2	3	4	5	
Energy	1	2	3	4	5	
Social Connections	1	2	3	4	5	

Win tomorrow today: Plan your top 3 priorities the night before or early in the morning.   For each activity, ask yourself "Is there a smarter way to achieve the same outcome?

"Simplicity boils down to two steps: Identify the essential. Eliminate the rest." – Leo Babauta

DAY: DAILY THEME:

Win the Day Planning

Today, I am grateful I get to be a coach because:

I have reviewed my team, recruiting, administrative & personal goals ☐

Today's Results List: List in priority order the top 3 things you can accomplish that would make a measurable impact on your goals and projects? What metric are you trying to hit? Schedule it.

Priority #1:   Metric I am aiming for_____

Priority #2:   Metric I am aiming for_____

Priority #3:   Metric I am aiming for_____

Person/People I need to Lead or Connect with Today (and How to Do It Well)

What or Who Am I Waiting On To Get a Project Done:

Who Needs Something From Me Today or This Week That I Can Proactively Get To Them?

○ **Morning Routine**   ○ **Workday Startup Routine**

TIME	DAILY SCHEDULE
5 am	
6 am	
7 am	
8 am	
9 am	
10 am	
11 am	
12 pm	
1 pm	
2 pm	
3 pm	
4 pm	
5 pm	
6 pm	
7 pm	
8 pm	
9 pm	
10 pm	
11 pm	

○ **Workday Shutdown Routine**   ○ **Evening Routine**

Staff meeting topics to cover:

Team meeting topics to cover:

THE DAILY TO-DO'S

Recruiting:	Administrative
Calls/texts to make:	
	Time Spent today
On Campus Visits:	Social Media:
Events to Recruit at:	
Time Spent today	Time Spent today
Team:	Personal:
Time Spent today	Time Spent today

PILE UP ZONE: Great ideas, goals, projects, apps or people to follow up on later

5 PERFORMANCE PILLARS	Give yourself a score of 1-5. 1=low and 5=high in terms of productivity					What could you do to get 1 point higher?
Mental Focus	1	2	3	4	5	
Mental/Emotional/Attitude	1	2	3	4	5	
Productivity	1	2	3	4	5	
Energy	1	2	3	4	5	
Social Connections	1	2	3	4	5	

Win tomorrow today: Plan your top 3 priorities the night before or early in the morning. For each activity, ask yourself "Is there a smarter way to achieve the same outcome?"

"Stop measuring days by degree of productivity and start experiencing them by degree of presence." – Alan Watts

DAY: DAILY THEME:

Win the Day Planning

Today, I am grateful I get to be a coach because:

I have reviewed my team, recruiting, administrative & personal goals ☐

Today's Results List: List in priority order the top 3 things you can accomplish that would make a measurable impact on your goals and projects? What metric are you trying to hit? Schedule it.

Priority #1:   **Metric I am aiming for_____**

Priority #2:   **Metric I am aiming for_____**

Priority #3:   **Metric I am aiming for_____**

Person/People I need to Lead or Connect with Today (and How to Do It Well)

What or Who Am I Waiting On To Get a Project Done:

Who Needs Something From Me Today or This Week That I Can Proactively Get To Them?

○ **Morning Routine**   ○ **Workday Startup Routine**

TIME	DAILY SCHEDULE
5 am	
6 am	
7 am	
8 am	
9 am	
10 am	
11 am	
12 pm	
1 pm	
2 pm	
3 pm	
4 pm	
5 pm	
6 pm	
7 pm	
8 pm	
9 pm	
10 pm	
11 pm	

○ **Workday Shutdown Routine**   ○ **Evening Routine**

Staff meeting topics to cover:

Team meeting topics to cover:

THE DAILY TO-DO'S

Recruiting:

Administrative

Calls/texts to make:

Time Spent today

On Campus Visits:

Social Media:

Events to Recruit at:

Time Spent today

Time Spent today

Team:

Personal:

Time Spent today

Time Spent today

PILE UP ZONE: Great ideas, goals, projects, apps or people to follow up on later

5 PERFORMANCE PILLARS	Give yourself a score of 1-5. 1=low and 5=high in terms of productivity					What could you do to get 1 point higher?
Mental Focus	1	2	3	4	5	
Mental/Emotional/Attitude	1	2	3	4	5	
Productivity	1	2	3	4	5	
Energy	1	2	3	4	5	
Social Connections	1	2	3	4	5	

Win tomorrow today: Plan your top 3 priorities the night before or early in the morning.   For each activity, ask yourself "Is there a smarter way to achieve the same outcome?"

"Strive not to be a success, but rather to be of value." – Albert Einstein

DAY: DAILY THEME:

Win the Day Planning

Today, I am grateful I get to be a coach because:

I have reviewed my team, recruiting, administrative & personal goals ☐

Today's Results List: List in priority order the top 3 things you can accomplish that would make a measurable impact on your goals and projects? What metric are you trying to hit? Schedule it.

Priority #1:   **Metric I am aiming for_____**

Priority #2:   **Metric I am aiming for_____**

Priority #3:   **Metric I am aiming for_____**

Person/People I need to Lead or Connect with Today (and How to Do It Well)

What or Who Am I Waiting On To Get a Project Done:

Who Needs Something From Me Today or This Week That I Can Proactively Get To Them?

○ **Morning Routine**   ○ **Workday Startup Routine**

TIME	DAILY SCHEDULE
5 am	
6 am	
7 am	
8 am	
9 am	
10 am	
11 am	
12 pm	
1 pm	
2 pm	
3 pm	
4 pm	
5 pm	
6 pm	
7 pm	
8 pm	
9 pm	
10 pm	
11 pm	

○ **Workday Shutdown Routine**   ○ **Evening Routine**

Staff meeting topics to cover:

Team meeting topics to cover:

THE DAILY TO-DO'S

Recruiting:

Calls/texts to make:

On Campus Visits:

Events to Recruit at:

Time Spent today

Administrative

Time Spent today

Social Media:

Time Spent today

Team:

Time Spent today

Personal:

Time Spent today

PILE UP ZONE: Great ideas, goals, projects, apps or people to follow up on later

5 PERFORMANCE PILLARS	Give yourself a score of 1-5, 1=low and 5=high in terms of productivity					What could you do to get 1 point higher?
Mental Focus	1	2	3	4	5	
Mental/Emotional/Attitude	1	2	3	4	5	
Productivity	1	2	3	4	5	
Energy	1	2	3	4	5	
Social Connections	1	2	3	4	5	

Win tomorrow today: Plan your top 3 priorities the night before or early in the morning. For each activity, ask yourself "Is there a smarter way to achieve the same outcome?

"The true price of anything you do is the amount of time you exchange for it."– Henry David Thoreau

79

DAY: _____   DAILY THEME: _____

Win the Day Planning

Today, I am grateful I get to be a coach because:

I have reviewed my team, recruiting, administrative & personal goals ☐

Today's Results List: List in priority order the top 3 things you can accomplish that would make a measurable impact on your goals and projects? What metric are you trying to hit? Schedule it.

Priority #1:   Metric I am aiming for_____

Priority #2:   Metric I am aiming for_____

Priority #3:   Metric I am aiming for_____

Person/People I need to Lead or Connect with Today (and How to Do It Well)

What or Who Am I Waiting On To Get a Project Done:

Who Needs Something From Me Today or This Week That I Can Proactively Get To Them?

○ **Morning Routine**   ○ **Workday Startup Routine**

TIME	DAILY SCHEDULE
5 am	
6 am	
7 am	
8 am	
9 am	
10 am	
11 am	
12 pm	
1 pm	
2 pm	
3 pm	
4 pm	
5 pm	
6 pm	
7 pm	
8 pm	
9 pm	
10 pm	
11 pm	

○ **Workday Shutdown Routine**   ○ **Evening Routine**

Staff meeting topics to cover:

Team meeting topics to cover:

THE DAILY TO-DO'S

Recruiting:

Calls/texts to make:

On Campus Visits:

Events to Recruit at:

| | Time Spent today |

Administrative

| | Time Spent today |

Social Media:

| | Time Spent today |

Team:

| | Time Spent today |

Personal:

| | Time Spent today |

PILE UP ZONE: Great ideas, goals, projects, apps or people to follow up on later

5 PERFORMANCE PILLARS	Give yourself a score of 1-5, 1=low and 5=high in terms of productivity					What could you do to get 1 point higher?
Mental Focus	1	2	3	4	5	
Mental/Emotional/Attitude	1	2	3	4	5	
Productivity	1	2	3	4	5	
Energy	1	2	3	4	5	
Social Connections	1	2	3	4	5	

Win tomorrow today: Plan your top 3 priorities the night before or early in the morning. For each activity, ask yourself "Is there a smarter way to achieve the same outcome?"

It is not enough to be busy, so are the ants. The question is: What are we busy about? – Henry David Thoreau

DAY: _____   DAILY THEME: _____

Win the Day Planning

Today, I am grateful I get to be a coach because:

I have reviewed my team, recruiting, administrative & personal goals ☐

Today's Results List: List in priority order the top 3 things you can accomplish that would make a measurable impact on your goals and projects? What metric are you trying to hit? Schedule it.

Priority #1:   **Metric I am aiming for_____**

Priority #2:   **Metric I am aiming for_____**

Priority #3:   **Metric I am aiming for_____**

Person/People I need to Lead or Connect with Today (and How to Do It Well)

What or Who Am I Waiting On To Get a Project Done:

Who Needs Something From Me Today or This Week That I Can Proactively Get To Them?

○ **Morning Routine**   ○ **Workday Startup Routine**

TIME	DAILY SCHEDULE
5 am	
6 am	
7 am	
8 am	
9 am	
10 am	
11 am	
12 pm	
1 pm	
2 pm	
3 pm	
4 pm	
5 pm	
6 pm	
7 pm	
8 pm	
9 pm	
10 pm	
11 pm	

○ **Workday Shutdown Routine**   ○ **Evening Routine**

Staff meeting topics to cover:

Team meeting topics to cover:

THE DAILY TO-DO'S

Recruiting:

Administrative

Calls/texts to make:

Time Spent today

On Campus Visits:

Social Media:

Events to Recruit at:

Time Spent today

Time Spent today

Team:

Personal:

Time Spent today

Time Spent today

PILE UP ZONE: Great ideas, goals, projects, apps or people to follow up on later

5 PERFORMANCE PILLARS	Give yourself a score of 1-5, 1=low and 5=high in terms of productivity					What could you do to get 1 point higher?
Mental Focus	1	2	3	4	5	
Mental/Emotional/Attitude	1	2	3	4	5	
Productivity	1	2	3	4	5	
Energy	1	2	3	4	5	
Social Connections	1	2	3	4	5	

Win tomorrow today: Plan your top 3 priorities the night before or early in the morning. For each activity, ask yourself "Is there a smarter way to achieve the same outcome?"

Are you busy being productive? – Anonymous

DAY: _____   DAILY THEME: _____

Win the Day Planning

Today, I am grateful I get to be a coach because:

I have reviewed my team, recruiting, administrative & personal goals ☐

Today's Results List: List in priority order the top 3 things you can accomplish that would make a measurable impact on your goals and projects? What metric are you trying to hit? Schedule it.

Priority #1:   **Metric I am aiming for_____**

Priority #2:   **Metric I am aiming for_____**

Priority #3:   **Metric I am aiming for_____**

Person/People I need to Lead or Connect with Today (and How to Do It Well)

What or Who Am I Waiting On To Get a Project Done:

Who Needs Something From Me Today or This Week That I Can Proactively Get To Them?

○ **Morning Routine**   ○ **Workday Startup Routine**

TIME	DAILY SCHEDULE
5 am	
6 am	
7 am	
8 am	
9 am	
10 am	
11 am	
12 pm	
1 pm	
2 pm	
3 pm	
4 pm	
5 pm	
6 pm	
7 pm	
8 pm	
9 pm	
10 pm	
11 pm	

○ **Workday Shutdown Routine**   ○ **Evening Routine**

Staff meeting topics to cover:

Team meeting topics to cover:

THE DAILY TO-DO'S

Recruiting:

Administrative

Calls/texts to make:

On Campus Visits:

Time Spent today

Social Media:

Events to Recruit at:

Time Spent today

Time Spent today

Team:

Personal:

Time Spent today

Time Spent today

PILE UP ZONE: Great ideas, goals, projects, apps or people to follow up on later

5 PERFORMANCE PILLARS	Give yourself a score of 1-5, 1=low and 5=high in terms of productivity					What could you do to get 1 point higher?
Mental Focus	1	2	3	4	5	
Mental/Emotional/Attitude	1	2	3	4	5	
Productivity	1	2	3	4	5	
Energy	1	2	3	4	5	
Social Connections	1	2	3	4	5	

Win tomorrow today: Plan your top 3 priorities the night before or early in the morning. For each activity, ask yourself "Is there a smarter way to achieve the same outcome?

The best way out is always through. – Robert Frost

DAY: DAILY THEME:

Win the Day Planning

Today, I am grateful I get to be a coach because:

I have reviewed my team, recruiting, administrative & personal goals ☐

Today's Results List: List in priority order the top 3 things you can accomplish that would make a measurable impact on your goals and projects? What metric are you trying to hit? Schedule it.

Priority #1: Metric I am aiming for_____

Priority #2: Metric I am aiming for_____

Priority #3: Metric I am aiming for_____

Person/People I need to Lead or Connect with Today (and How to Do It Well)

What or Who Am I Waiting On To Get a Project Done:

Who Needs Something From Me Today or This Week That I Can Proactively Get To Them?

○ **Morning Routine**   ○ **Workday Startup Routine**

TIME	DAILY SCHEDULE
5 am	
6 am	
7 am	
8 am	
9 am	
10 am	
11 am	
12 pm	
1 pm	
2 pm	
3 pm	
4 pm	
5 pm	
6 pm	
7 pm	
8 pm	
9 pm	
10 pm	
11 pm	

○ **Workday Shutdown Routine**   ○ **Evening Routine**

Staff meeting topics to cover:

Team meeting topics to cover:

THE DAILY TO-DO'S

Recruiting:

Administrative

Calls/texts to make:

Time Spent today

On Campus Visits:

Social Media:

Events to Recruit at:

Time Spent today

Time Spent today

Team:

Personal:

Time Spent today

Time Spent today

PILE UP ZONE: Great ideas, goals, projects, apps or people to follow up on later

5 PERFORMANCE PILLARS	Give yourself a score of 1-5, 1=low and 5=high in terms of productivity					What could you do to get 1 point higher?
Mental Focus	1	2	3	4	5	
Mental/Emotional/Attitude	1	2	3	4	5	
Productivity	1	2	3	4	5	
Energy	1	2	3	4	5	
Social Connections	1	2	3	4	5	

Win tomorrow today: Plan your top 3 priorities the night before or early in the morning. For each activity, ask yourself "Is there a smarter way to achieve the same outcome?

Action is the foundational key to all success. – Picasso

DAY: DAILY THEME:

Win the Day Planning		

Today, I am grateful I get to be a coach because:

I have reviewed my team, recruiting, administrative & personal goals ☐

Today's Results List: List in priority order the top 3 things you can accomplish that would make a measurable impact on your goals and projects? What metric are you trying to hit? Schedule it.

Priority #1:   Metric I am aiming for_____

Priority #2:   Metric I am aiming for_____

Priority #3:   Metric I am aiming for_____

○ **Morning Routine**   ○ **Workday Startup Routine**

TIME	DAILY SCHEDULE
5 am	
6 am	
7 am	
8 am	
9 am	
10 am	
11 am	
12 pm	
1 pm	
2 pm	
3 pm	
4 pm	
5 pm	
6 pm	
7 pm	
8 pm	
9 pm	
10 pm	
11 pm	

○ **Workday Shutdown Routine**   ○ **Evening Routine**

Person/People I need to Lead or Connect with Today (and How to Do It Well)

Staff meeting topics to cover:

What or Who Am I Waiting On To Get a Project Done:

Team meeting topics to cover:

Who Needs Something From Me Today or This Week That I Can Proactively Get To Them?

THE DAILY TO-DO'S

Recruiting:

Administrative

Calls/texts to make:

Time Spent today

On Campus Visits:

Social Media:

Events to Recruit at:

Time Spent today

Time Spent today

Team:

Personal:

Time Spent today

Time Spent today

PILE UP ZONE: Great ideas, goals, projects, apps or people to follow up on later

5 PERFORMANCE PILLARS	Give yourself a score of 1-5, 1=low and 5=high in terms of productivity					What could you do to get 1 point higher?
Mental Focus	1	2	3	4	5	
Mental/Emotional/Attitude	1	2	3	4	5	
Productivity	1	2	3	4	5	
Energy	1	2	3	4	5	
Social Connections	1	2	3	4	5	

Win tomorrow today: Plan your top 3 priorities the night before or early in the morning. For each activity, ask yourself "Is there a smarter way to achieve the same outcome?

Stressing output is the key to improving productivity, while looking to increase activity can result in just the opposite. — Paul Gauguin

4 WEEK - PLAN, DO, REVIEW, AND IMPROVE THE SYSTEM

Here is your chance to reflect back on the last month and see...

What should I/we stop doing? What should I/we do less? What should I/we continue doing? What should I/we do more? What should I/we start doing?

Reflect back on your activities to track and see your progress, notice patterns and review your accomplishments, gives you the opportunity to adjust, re-invent and plan your next 4 weeks.

The cycle is: Do the work → Look back → Look forward → Plan the next 4 weeks → Do the work...

	What Should I/We Stop Doing?	What Should I/We Do Less?	What Should I/We Continue Doing?	What Should I/we Do More Of?	What Should I/We Start Doing?
Recruiting Goals, Processes, Daily Activities					
Team Goals, Projects, Daily Activities					
Administrative Goals, Projects, Daily Activities					
Personal Goals, Projects, Daily Activities					
5 Performance Pillars					

4 WEEK SPRINT - PLAN, DO, REVIEW, AND IMPROVE THE SYSTEM

TIME AUDIT:

	Actual Time Spent	Ideal Time Spent	Adjustments to make:
Recruiting			
Team			
Administrative			
Social Media			
Personal			

3 big wins over the last 30 days were . . .

My biggest struggle over the last 30 days was. . .

. .and if I were advising or mentoring someone dealing with the same struggle, I'd advise them to . . .

4 WEEK PERFORMANCE REVIEW

Score yourself on a scale of 1 to 5 in each of the areas below, with 5 being the best. Also, write any notes in the bubbles about what is happening in that area or what you would like to improve. Be honest, but also be kind to yourself. Tally your scores up and multiply by 2, and that will give you a score out of 100. Basically, you're doing a spot check on your life and giving yourself a score so that you know where you are.

RECRUITING	ADMINISTRATIVE	TEAM/STAFF	SOCIAL MEDIA	PRODUCTIVITY
Score 1-5_____	Score 1-5_____	Score 1-5_____	Score 1-5_____	Score 1-5_____

HEALTH/ENERGY	MENTAL/EMOTIONAL	FAMILY	FRIENDS	FOCUS
Score 1-5_____	Score 1-5_____	Score 1-5_____	Score 1-5_____	Score 1-5_____

MONTH / YEAR:

THEME:

FOCUS AREAS FOR GROWTH AND IMPROVEMENT THIS MONTH	✓
1.	○
2.	○
3.	○

STRATEGIES/PROJECTS TO HELP REACH GOALS

Establish 1-2 projects that are going to help you reach the goals you listed above.

SUNDAY	MONDAY	TUESDAY

Major Events

Write down any major events coming up this month, and how you can prepare for them.

These things MUST happen this month

How do you build your program exponentially in a relatively short amount of time? Through focus. Use this section in each area to drive the direction of your month, week, and day to eliminate activities that just do NOT fit in. Always refer back to your focus and ask yourself..."Am I working on things that support my focus?"

WEDNESDAY	THURSDAY	FRIDAY	SATURDAY

Recruiting deadlines/outcomes we need this month Include:	The best ways I can prepare and ensure that I show up to win this month are:

YOUR IDEAL WEEK

Day Themes

FOCUS AREA FOR GROWTH AND IMPROVEMENT THIS WEEK	✓
1.	○
2.	○
3.	○

Focus Areas

TIME	MONDAY	TUESDAY	WEDNESDAY
5:00 - 5:30 AM			
6:00 - 6:30 AM			
7:00 - 7:30 AM			
8:00 - 8:30 AM			
9:00 - 9:30 AM			
10:00 - 10:30 AM			
11:00 - 11:30 AM			
12:00 - 12:30 PM			
1:00 - 1:30 PM			
2:00 - 2:30 PM			
3:00 - 3:30 PM			
4:00 - 4:30 PM			
5:00 - 5:30 PM			
6:00 - 6:30 PM			
7:00 - 7:30 PM			
8:00 - 8:30 PM			
9:00 - 9:30 PM			
10:00 - 10:30 PM			
11:00 - 11:30 PM			
12:00 - 12:30 AM			

HOW TO SCHEDULE YOUR IDEAL WEEK

Make time for what matters first.

Note on this calendar when you will have:

1. Family time
2. Weekly reflection
3. Self-care time
4. Wake up time
5. Go to bed time
6. Work stop time
7. Practice
8. Weights
9. Meetings
10. After all of this is set, what big blocks of time to do you have left for the growth and improvement projects you listed above? Find at least 1 hour each day and block it off.
11. Fit all of the busy work in between your blocks of program building projects.

Last week's wins & lessons learned:

USE THIS PAGE TO CREATE AN OVERVIEW FOR NEXT WEEK

THURSDAY	FRIDAY	SATURDAY	SUNDAY

Thoughts for this upcoming week:

DAY: _____   DAILY THEME: _____

Win the Day Planning

Today, I am grateful I get to be a coach because:

I have reviewed my team, recruiting, administrative & personal goals ☐

Today's Results List: List in priority order the top 3 things you can accomplish that would make a measurable impact on your goals and projects? What metric are you trying to hit? Schedule it.

Priority #1:   Metric I am aiming for_____

Priority #2:   Metric I am aiming for_____

Priority #3:   Metric I am aiming for_____

Person/People I need to Lead or Connect with Today (and How to Do It Well)

What or Who Am I Waiting On To Get a Project Done:

Who Needs Something From Me Today or This Week That I Can Proactively Get To Them?

○ **Morning Routine**   ○ **Workday Startup Routine**

TIME	DAILY SCHEDULE
5 am	
6 am	
7 am	
8 am	
9 am	
10 am	
11 am	
12 pm	
1 pm	
2 pm	
3 pm	
4 pm	
5 pm	
6 pm	
7 pm	
8 pm	
9 pm	
10 pm	
11 pm	

○ **Workday Shutdown Routine**   ○ **Evening Routine**

Staff meeting topics to cover:

Team meeting topics to cover:

THE DAILY TO-DO'S

Recruiting:

Calls/texts to make:

On Campus Visits:

Events to Recruit at:

Time Spent today

Team:

Time Spent today

Administrative

Time Spent today

Social Media:

Time Spent today

Personal:

Time Spent today

PILE UP ZONE: Great ideas, goals, projects, apps or people to follow up on later

5 PERFORMANCE PILLARS	Give yourself a score of 1-5, 1=low and 5=high in terms of productivity					What could you do to get 1 point higher?
Mental Focus	1	2	3	4	5	
Mental/Emotional/Attitude	1	2	3	4	5	
Productivity	1	2	3	4	5	
Energy	1	2	3	4	5	
Social Connections	1	2	3	4	5	

Win tomorrow today: Plan your top 3 priorities the night before or early in the morning. For each activity, ask yourself "Is there a smarter way to achieve the same outcome?

You can't get much done in life if you only work on days when you feel good. – Jerry West

DAY: DAILY THEME:

Win the Day Planning

Today, I am grateful I get to be a coach because:

I have reviewed my team, recruiting, administrative & personal goals ☐

Today's Results List: List in priority order the top 3 things you can accomplish that would make a measurable impact on your goals and projects? What metric are you trying to hit? Schedule it.

Priority #1:   Metric I am aiming for_____

Priority #2:   Metric I am aiming for_____

Priority #3:   Metric I am aiming for_____

○ **Morning Routine**   ○ **Workday Startup Routine**

TIME	DAILY SCHEDULE
5 am	
6 am	
7 am	
8 am	
9 am	
10 am	
11 am	
12 pm	
1 pm	
2 pm	
3 pm	
4 pm	
5 pm	
6 pm	
7 pm	
8 pm	
9 pm	
10 pm	
11 pm	

○ **Workday Shutdown Routine**   ○ **Evening Routine**

Person/People I need to Lead or Connect with Today (and How to Do It Well)

Staff meeting topics to cover:

What or Who Am I Waiting On To Get a Project Done:

Team meeting topics to cover:

Who Needs Something From Me Today or This Week That I Can Proactively Get To Them?

THE DAILY TO-DO'S

Recruiting:

Calls/texts to make:

On Campus Visits:

Events to Recruit at:

Time Spent today

Team:

Time Spent today

Administrative

Time Spent today

Social Media:

Time Spent today

Personal:

Time Spent today

PILE UP ZONE: Great ideas, goals, projects, apps or people to follow up on later

5 PERFORMANCE PILLARS	Give yourself a score of 1-5, 1=low and 5=high in terms of productivity					What could you do to get 1 point higher?
Mental Focus	1	2	3	4	5	
Mental/Emotional/Attitude	1	2	3	4	5	
Productivity	1	2	3	4	5	
Energy	1	2	3	4	5	
Social Connections	1	2	3	4	5	

Win tomorrow today: Plan your top 3 priorities the night before or early in the morning. For each activity, ask yourself "Is there a smarter way to achieve the same outcome?

Busy is a decision – Debbie Millman

DAY: DAILY THEME:

| Win the Day Planning | | ○ **Morning Routine**   ○ **Workday Startup Routine** |

Win the Day Planning

Today, I am grateful I get to be a coach because:

I have reviewed my team, recruiting, administrative & personal goals ☐

Today's Results List: List in priority order the top 3 things you can accomplish that would make a measurable impact on your goals and projects? What metric are you trying to hit? Schedule it.

Priority #1:   **Metric I am aiming for_____**

Priority #2:   **Metric I am aiming for_____**

Priority #3:   **Metric I am aiming for_____**

○ **Morning Routine**   ○ **Workday Startup Routine**

TIME	DAILY SCHEDULE
5 am	
6 am	
7 am	
8 am	
9 am	
10 am	
11 am	
12 pm	
1 pm	
2 pm	
3 pm	
4 pm	
5 pm	
6 pm	
7 pm	
8 pm	
9 pm	
10 pm	
11 pm	

○ **Workday Shutdown Routine**   ○ **Evening Routine**

Person/People I need to Lead or Connect with Today (and How to Do It Well)

Staff meeting topics to cover:

What or Who Am I Waiting On To Get a Project Done:

Team meeting topics to cover:

Who Needs Something From Me Today or This Week That I Can Proactively Get To Them?

THE DAILY TO-DO'S

Recruiting:

Calls/texts to make:

On Campus Visits:

Events to Recruit at:

Time Spent today

Administrative

Time Spent today

Social Media:

Time Spent today

Team:

Time Spent today

Personal:

Time Spent today

PILE UP ZONE: Great ideas, goals, projects, apps or people to follow up on later

5 PERFORMANCE PILLARS	Give yourself a score of 1-5, 1=low and 5=high in terms of productivity					What could you do to get 1 point higher?
Mental Focus	1	2	3	4	5	
Mental/Emotional/Attitude	1	2	3	4	5	
Productivity	1	2	3	4	5	
Energy	1	2	3	4	5	
Social Connections	1	2	3	4	5	

Win tomorrow today: Plan your top 3 priorities the night before or early in the morning. For each activity, ask yourself "Is there a smarter way to achieve the same outcome?

Just do what works for you because there will always be someone who thinks differently – Michelle Obama

DAY: DAILY THEME:

Win the Day Planning

Today, I am grateful I get to be a coach because:

I have reviewed my team, recruiting, administrative & personal goals ☐

Today's Results List: List in priority order the top 3 things you can accomplish that would make a measurable impact on your goals and projects? What metric are you trying to hit? Schedule it.

Priority #1:   Metric I am aiming for_____

Priority #2:   Metric I am aiming for_____

Priority #3:   Metric I am aiming for_____

Person/People I need to Lead or Connect with Today (and How to Do It Well)

What or Who Am I Waiting On To Get a Project Done:

Who Needs Something From Me Today or This Week That I Can Proactively Get To Them?

○ **Morning Routine**   ○ **Workday Startup Routine**

TIME	DAILY SCHEDULE
5 am	
6 am	
7 am	
8 am	
9 am	
10 am	
11 am	
12 pm	
1 pm	
2 pm	
3 pm	
4 pm	
5 pm	
6 pm	
7 pm	
8 pm	
9 pm	
10 pm	
11 pm	

○ **Workday Shutdown Routine**   ○ **Evening Routine**

Staff meeting topics to cover:

Team meeting topics to cover:

THE DAILY TO-DO'S

Recruiting:

Calls/texts to make:

On Campus Visits:

Events to Recruit at:

Time Spent today

Team:

Time Spent today

Administrative

Time Spent today

Social Media:

Time Spent today

Personal:

Time Spent today

PILE UP ZONE: Great ideas, goals, projects, apps or people to follow up on later

5 PERFORMANCE PILLARS	Give yourself a score of 1-5, 1=low and 5=high in terms of productivity					What could you do to get 1 point higher?
Mental Focus	1	2	3	4	5	
Mental/Emotional/Attitude	1	2	3	4	5	
Productivity	1	2	3	4	5	
Energy	1	2	3	4	5	
Social Connections	1	2	3	4	5	

Win tomorrow today: Plan your top 3 priorities the night before or early in the morning. For each activity, ask yourself "Is there a smarter way to achieve the same outcome?

"If you love life, don't waste time, for time is what life is made up of." – Bruce Lee

DAY: _____   DAILY THEME: _____

Win the Day Planning	

Today, I am grateful I get to be a coach because:

I have reviewed my team, recruiting, administrative & personal goals ☐

Today's Results List: List in priority order the top 3 things you can accomplish that would make a measurable impact on your goals and projects? What metric are you trying to hit? Schedule it.

Priority #1:   Metric I am aiming for_____

Priority #2:   Metric I am aiming for_____

Priority #3:   Metric I am aiming for_____

Person/People I need to Lead or Connect with Today (and How to Do It Well)

What or Who Am I Waiting On To Get a Project Done:

Who Needs Something From Me Today or This Week That I Can Proactively Get To Them?

○ **Morning Routine**   ○ **Workday Startup Routine**

TIME	DAILY SCHEDULE
5 am	
6 am	
7 am	
8 am	
9 am	
10 am	
11 am	
12 pm	
1 pm	
2 pm	
3 pm	
4 pm	
5 pm	
6 pm	
7 pm	
8 pm	
9 pm	
10 pm	
11 pm	

○ **Workday Shutdown Routine**   ○ **Evening Routine**

Staff meeting topics to cover:

Team meeting topics to cover:

THE DAILY TO-DO'S

Recruiting:

Calls/texts to make:

On Campus Visits:

Events to Recruit at:

Time Spent today

Team:

Time Spent today

Administrative

Time Spent today

Social Media:

Time Spent today

Personal:

Time Spent today

PILE UP ZONE: Great ideas, goals, projects, apps or people to follow up on later

5 PERFORMANCE PILLARS	Give yourself a score of 1-5, 1=low and 5=high in terms of productivity					What could you do to get 1 point higher?
Mental Focus	1	2	3	4	5	
Mental/Emotional/Attitude	1	2	3	4	5	
Productivity	1	2	3	4	5	
Energy	1	2	3	4	5	
Social Connections	1	2	3	4	5	

Win tomorrow today: Plan your top 3 priorities the night before or early in the morning. For each activity, ask yourself "Is there a smarter way to achieve the same outcome?

"The path to success is to take massive, determined action." – Tony Robbins

DAY: DAILY THEME:

Win the Day Planning

Today, I am grateful I get to be a coach because:

I have reviewed my team, recruiting, administrative & personal goals ☐

Today's Results List: List in priority order the top 3 things you can accomplish that would make a measurable impact on your goals and projects? What metric are you trying to hit? Schedule it.

Priority #1:   **Metric I am aiming for_____**

Priority #2:   **Metric I am aiming for_____**

Priority #3:   **Metric I am aiming for_____**

Person/People I need to Lead or Connect with Today (and How to Do It Well)

What or Who Am I Waiting On To Get a Project Done:

Who Needs Something From Me Today or This Week That I Can Proactively Get To Them?

○ **Morning Routine**   ○ **Workday Startup Routine**

TIME	DAILY SCHEDULE
5 am	
6 am	
7 am	
8 am	
9 am	
10 am	
11 am	
12 pm	
1 pm	
2 pm	
3 pm	
4 pm	
5 pm	
6 pm	
7 pm	
8 pm	
9 pm	
10 pm	
11 pm	

○ **Workday Shutdown Routine**   ○ **Evening Routine**

Staff meeting topics to cover:

Team meeting topics to cover:

THE DAILY TO-DO'S

Recruiting:

Administrative

Calls/texts to make:

Time Spent today

On Campus Visits:

Social Media:

Events to Recruit at:

Time Spent today

Time Spent today

Team:

Personal:

Time Spent today

Time Spent today

PILE UP ZONE: Great ideas, goals, projects, apps or people to follow up on later

5 PERFORMANCE PILLARS	Give yourself a score of 1-5. 1=low and 5=high in terms of productivity					What could you do to get 1 point higher?
Mental Focus	1	2	3	4	5	
Mental/Emotional/Attitude	1	2	3	4	5	
Productivity	1	2	3	4	5	
Energy	1	2	3	4	5	
Social Connections	1	2	3	4	5	

Win tomorrow today: Plan your top 3 priorities the night before or early in the morning. For each activity, ask yourself "Is there a smarter way to achieve the same outcome?"

"It's not knowing what to do, it's doing what you know." --Tony Robbins

DAY: DAILY THEME:

Win the Day Planning	

Today, I am grateful I get to be a coach because:

I have reviewed my team, recruiting, administrative & personal goals ☐

Today's Results List: List in priority order the top 3 things you can accomplish that would make a measurable impact on your goals and projects? What metric are you trying to hit? Schedule it.

Priority #1:   Metric I am aiming for_____

Priority #2:   Metric I am aiming for_____

Priority #3:   Metric I am aiming for_____

○ **Morning Routine**   ○ **Workday Startup Routine**

TIME	DAILY SCHEDULE
5 am	
6 am	
7 am	
8 am	
9 am	
10 am	
11 am	
12 pm	
1 pm	
2 pm	
3 pm	
4 pm	
5 pm	
6 pm	
7 pm	
8 pm	
9 pm	
10 pm	
11 pm	

○ **Workday Shutdown Routine**   ○ **Evening Routine**

Person/People I need to Lead or Connect with Today (and How to Do It Well)

Staff meeting topics to cover:

What or Who Am I Waiting On To Get a Project Done:

Team meeting topics to cover:

Who Needs Something From Me Today or This Week That I Can Proactively Get To Them?

THE DAILY TO-DO'S

Recruiting:

Administrative

Calls/texts to make:

Time Spent today

On Campus Visits:

Social Media:

Events to Recruit at:

Time Spent today

Time Spent today

Team:

Personal:

Time Spent today

Time Spent today

PILE UP ZONE: Great ideas, goals, projects, apps or people to follow up on later

5 PERFORMANCE PILLARS	Give yourself a score of 1-5, 1=low and 5=high in terms of productivity					What could you do to get 1 point higher?
Mental Focus	1	2	3	4	5	
Mental/Emotional/Attitude	1	2	3	4	5	
Productivity	1	2	3	4	5	
Energy	1	2	3	4	5	
Social Connections	1	2	3	4	5	

Win tomorrow today: Plan your top 3 priorities the night before or early in the morning. For each activity, ask yourself "Is there a smarter way to achieve the same outcome?"

"The key is not to prioritize what's on your schedule, but to schedule your priorities." --Stephen Covey

DAY: DAILY THEME:

Win the Day Planning

Today, I am grateful I get to be a coach because:

I have reviewed my team, recruiting, administrative & personal goals ☐

Today's Results List: List in priority order the top 3 things you can accomplish that would make a measurable impact on your goals and projects? What metric are you trying to hit? Schedule it.

Priority #1:   Metric I am aiming for_____

Priority #2:   Metric I am aiming for_____

Priority #3:   Metric I am aiming for_____

○ **Morning Routine**   ○ **Workday Startup Routine**

TIME	DAILY SCHEDULE
5 am	
6 am	
7 am	
8 am	
9 am	
10 am	
11 am	
12 pm	
1 pm	
2 pm	
3 pm	
4 pm	
5 pm	
6 pm	
7 pm	
8 pm	
9 pm	
10 pm	
11 pm	

○ **Workday Shutdown Routine**   ○ **Evening Routine**

Person/People I need to Lead or Connect with Today (and How to Do It Well)

Staff meeting topics to cover:

What or Who Am I Waiting On To Get a Project Done:

Team meeting topics to cover:

Who Needs Something From Me Today or This Week That I Can Proactively Get To Them?

THE DAILY TO-DO'S

Recruiting:	Administrative
Calls/texts to make:	
	Time Spent today
On Campus Visits:	Social Media:
Events to Recruit at:	
Time Spent today	Time Spent today
Team:	Personal:
Time Spent today	Time Spent today

PILE UP ZONE: Great ideas, goals, projects, apps or people to follow up on later

5 PERFORMANCE PILLARS	Give yourself a score of 1-5. 1=low and 5=high in terms of productivity					What could you do to get 1 point higher?
Mental Focus	1	2	3	4	5	
Mental/Emotional/Attitude	1	2	3	4	5	
Productivity	1	2	3	4	5	
Energy	1	2	3	4	5	
Social Connections	1	2	3	4	5	

Win tomorrow today: Plan your top 3 priorities the night before or early in the morning. For each activity, ask yourself "Is there a smarter way to achieve the same outcome?

"Ordinary people think merely of spending time, great people think of using it." --Arthur Schopenhauer

111

DAY: DAILY THEME:

Win the Day Planning

Today, I am grateful I get to be a coach because:

I have reviewed my team, recruiting, administrative & personal goals ☐

Today's Results List: List in priority order the top 3 things you can accomplish that would make a measurable impact on your goals and projects? What metric are you trying to hit? Schedule it.

Priority #1:   **Metric I am aiming for_____**

Priority #2:   **Metric I am aiming for_____**

Priority #3:   **Metric I am aiming for_____**

Person/People I need to Lead or Connect with Today (and How to Do It Well)

What or Who Am I Waiting On To Get a Project Done:

Who Needs Something From Me Today or This Week That I Can Proactively Get To Them?

○ **Morning Routine**   ○ **Workday Startup Routine**

TIME	DAILY SCHEDULE
5 am	
6 am	
7 am	
8 am	
9 am	
10 am	
11 am	
12 pm	
1 pm	
2 pm	
3 pm	
4 pm	
5 pm	
6 pm	
7 pm	
8 pm	
9 pm	
10 pm	
11 pm	

○ **Workday Shutdown Routine**   ○ **Evening Routine**

Staff meeting topics to cover:

Team meeting topics to cover:

THE DAILY TO-DO'S

Recruiting:

Administrative

Calls/texts to make:

Time Spent today

On Campus Visits:

Social Media:

Events to Recruit at:

Time Spent today

Time Spent today

Team:

Personal:

Time Spent today

Time Spent today

PILE UP ZONE: Great ideas, goals, projects, apps or people to follow up on later

5 PERFORMANCE PILLARS	Give yourself a score of 1-5, 1=low and 5=high in terms of productivity					What could you do to get 1 point higher?
Mental Focus	1	2	3	4	5	
Mental/Emotional/Attitude	1	2	3	4	5	
Productivity	1	2	3	4	5	
Energy	1	2	3	4	5	
Social Connections	1	2	3	4	5	

Win tomorrow today: Plan your top 3 priorities the night before or early in the morning. For each activity, ask yourself "Is there a smarter way to achieve the same outcome?

"Your mind is for having ideas, not holding them." --David Allen

DAY: DAILY THEME:

Win the Day Planning

Today, I am grateful I get to be a coach because:

I have reviewed my team, recruiting, administrative & personal goals ☐

Today's Results List: List in priority order the top 3 things you can accomplish that would make a measurable impact on your goals and projects? What metric are you trying to hit? Schedule it.

Priority #1:   **Metric I am aiming for_____**

Priority #2:   **Metric I am aiming for_____**

Priority #3:   **Metric I am aiming for_____**

Person/People I need to Lead or Connect with Today (and How to Do It Well)

What or Who Am I Waiting On To Get a Project Done:

Who Needs Something From Me Today or This Week That I Can Proactively Get To Them?

○ **Morning Routine**   ○ **Workday Startup Routine**

TIME	DAILY SCHEDULE
5 am	
6 am	
7 am	
8 am	
9 am	
10 am	
11 am	
12 pm	
1 pm	
2 pm	
3 pm	
4 pm	
5 pm	
6 pm	
7 pm	
8 pm	
9 pm	
10 pm	
11 pm	

○ **Workday Shutdown Routine**   ○ **Evening Routine**

Staff meeting topics to cover:

Team meeting topics to cover:

THE DAILY TO-DO'S

Recruiting:

Calls/texts to make:

On Campus Visits:

Events to Recruit at:

Time Spent today

Team:

Time Spent today

Administrative

Time Spent today

Social Media:

Time Spent today

Personal:

Time Spent today

PILE UP ZONE: Great ideas, goals, projects, apps or people to follow up on later

5 PERFORMANCE PILLARS	Give yourself a score of 1-5, 1=low and 5=high in terms of productivity					What could you do to get 1 point higher?
Mental Focus	1	2	3	4	5	
Mental/Emotional/Attitude	1	2	3	4	5	
Productivity	1	2	3	4	5	
Energy	1	2	3	4	5	
Social Connections	1	2	3	4	5	

Win tomorrow today: Plan your top 3 priorities the night before or early in the morning. For each activity, ask yourself "Is there a smarter way to achieve the same outcome?"

"Success is often achieved by those who don't know that failure is inevitable." --Coco Chanel

DAY: DAILY THEME:

	Win the Day Planning

Today, I am grateful I get to be a coach because:

I have reviewed my team, recruiting, administrative & personal goals ☐

Today's Results List: List in priority order the top 3 things you can accomplish that would make a measurable impact on your goals and projects? What metric are you trying to hit? Schedule it.

Priority #1:   **Metric I am aiming for_____**

Priority #2:   **Metric I am aiming for_____**

Priority #3:   **Metric I am aiming for_____**

Person/People I need to Lead or Connect with Today (and How to Do It Well)

What or Who Am I Waiting On To Get a Project Done:

Who Needs Something From Me Today or This Week That I Can Proactively Get To Them?

○ **Morning Routine**   ○ **Workday Startup Routine**

TIME	DAILY SCHEDULE
5 am	
6 am	
7 am	
8 am	
9 am	
10 am	
11 am	
12 pm	
1 pm	
2 pm	
3 pm	
4 pm	
5 pm	
6 pm	
7 pm	
8 pm	
9 pm	
10 pm	
11 pm	

○ **Workday Shutdown Routine**   ○ **Evening Routine**

Staff meeting topics to cover:

Team meeting topics to cover:

THE DAILY TO-DO'S

Recruiting:

Calls/texts to make:

On Campus Visits:

Events to Recruit at:

Time Spent today

Administrative

Time Spent today

Social Media:

Time Spent today

Team:

Time Spent today

Personal:

Time Spent today

PILE UP ZONE: Great ideas, goals, projects, apps or people to follow up on later

5 PERFORMANCE PILLARS	Give yourself a score of 1-5, 1=low and 5=high in terms of productivity					What could you do to get 1 point higher?
Mental Focus	1	2	3	4	5	
Mental/Emotional/Attitude	1	2	3	4	5	
Productivity	1	2	3	4	5	
Energy	1	2	3	4	5	
Social Connections	1	2	3	4	5	

Win tomorrow today: Plan your top 3 priorities the night before or early in the morning. For each activity, ask yourself "Is there a smarter way to achieve the same outcome?

"It's not always that we need to do more but rather that we need to focus on less." --Nathan W. Morris

DAY: DAILY THEME:

Win the Day Planning

Today, I am grateful I get to be a coach because:

I have reviewed my team, recruiting, administrative & personal goals ☐

Today's Results List: List in priority order the top 3 things you can accomplish that would make a measurable impact on your goals and projects? What metric are you trying to hit? Schedule it.

Priority #1:   **Metric I am aiming for_____**

Priority #2:   **Metric I am aiming for_____**

Priority #3:   **Metric I am aiming for_____**

○ **Morning Routine**   ○ **Workday Startup Routine**

TIME	DAILY SCHEDULE
5 am	
6 am	
7 am	
8 am	
9 am	
10 am	
11 am	
12 pm	
1 pm	
2 pm	
3 pm	
4 pm	
5 pm	
6 pm	
7 pm	
8 pm	
9 pm	
10 pm	
11 pm	

○ **Workday Shutdown Routine**   ○ **Evening Routine**

Person/People I need to Lead or Connect with Today (and How to Do It Well)

Staff meeting topics to cover:

What or Who Am I Waiting On To Get a Project Done:

Team meeting topics to cover:

Who Needs Something From Me Today or This Week That I Can Proactively Get To Them?

118

THE DAILY TO-DO'S

Recruiting:

Administrative

Calls/texts to make:

Time Spent today

On Campus Visits:

Social Media:

Events to Recruit at:

Time Spent today

Time Spent today

Team:

Personal:

Time Spent today

Time Spent today

PILE UP ZONE: Great ideas, goals, projects, apps or people to follow up on later

5 PERFORMANCE PILLARS	Give yourself a score of 1-5, 1=low and 5=high in terms of productivity					What could you do to get 1 point higher?
Mental Focus	1	2	3	4	5	
Mental/Emotional/Attitude	1	2	3	4	5	
Productivity	1	2	3	4	5	
Energy	1	2	3	4	5	
Social Connections	1	2	3	4	5	

Win tomorrow today: Plan your top 3 priorities the night before or early in the morning. For each activity, ask yourself "Is there a smarter way to achieve the same outcome?

"Great acts are made up of small deeds." --Lao Tzu

DAY: DAILY THEME:

Win the Day Planning

Today, I am grateful I get to be a coach because:

I have reviewed my team, recruiting, administrative & personal goals ☐

Today's Results List: List in priority order the top 3 things you can accomplish that would make a measurable impact on your goals and projects? What metric are you trying to hit? Schedule it.

Priority #1:   Metric I am aiming for_____

Priority #2:   Metric I am aiming for_____

Priority #3:   Metric I am aiming for_____

Person/People I need to Lead or Connect with Today (and How to Do It Well)

What or Who Am I Waiting On To Get a Project Done:

Who Needs Something From Me Today or This Week That I Can Proactively Get To Them?

○ **Morning Routine**   ○ **Workday Startup Routine**

TIME	DAILY SCHEDULE
5 am	
6 am	
7 am	
8 am	
9 am	
10 am	
11 am	
12 pm	
1 pm	
2 pm	
3 pm	
4 pm	
5 pm	
6 pm	
7 pm	
8 pm	
9 pm	
10 pm	
11 pm	

○ **Workday Shutdown Routine**   ○ **Evening Routine**

Staff meeting topics to cover:

Team meeting topics to cover:

THE DAILY TO-DO'S

Recruiting:

Calls/texts to make:

On Campus Visits:

Events to Recruit at:

Time Spent today

Administrative

Time Spent today

Social Media:

Time Spent today

Team:

Time Spent today

Personal:

Time Spent today

PILE UP ZONE: Great ideas, goals, projects, apps or people to follow up on later

5 PERFORMANCE PILLARS	Give yourself a score of 1-5, 1=low and 5=high in terms of productivity					What could you do to get 1 point higher?
Mental Focus	1	2	3	4	5	
Mental/Emotional/Attitude	1	2	3	4	5	
Productivity	1	2	3	4	5	
Energy	1	2	3	4	5	
Social Connections	1	2	3	4	5	

Win tomorrow today: Plan your top 3 priorities the night before or early in the morning.   For each activity, ask yourself "Is there a smarter way to achieve the same outcome?

"Don't wait. The time will never be just right." --Napoleon Hill

121

DAY: DAILY THEME:

Win the Day Planning

Today, I am grateful I get to be a coach because:

I have reviewed my team, recruiting, administrative & personal goals ☐

Today's Results List: List in priority order the top 3 things you can accomplish that would make a measurable impact on your goals and projects? What metric are you trying to hit? Schedule it.

Priority #1:   **Metric I am aiming for_____**

Priority #2:   **Metric I am aiming for_____**

Priority #3:   **Metric I am aiming for_____**

Person/People I need to Lead or Connect with Today (and How to Do It Well)

What or Who Am I Waiting On To Get a Project Done:

Who Needs Something From Me Today or This Week That I Can Proactively Get To Them?

○ **Morning Routine**   ○ **Workday Startup Routine**

TIME	DAILY SCHEDULE
5 am	
6 am	
7 am	
8 am	
9 am	
10 am	
11 am	
12 pm	
1 pm	
2 pm	
3 pm	
4 pm	
5 pm	
6 pm	
7 pm	
8 pm	
9 pm	
10 pm	
11 pm	

○ **Workday Shutdown Routine**   ○ **Evening Routine**

Staff meeting topics to cover:

Team meeting topics to cover:

THE DAILY TO-DO'S

Recruiting:

Administrative

Calls/texts to make:

Time Spent today

On Campus Visits:

Social Media:

Events to Recruit at:

Time Spent today

Time Spent today

Team:

Personal:

Time Spent today

Time Spent today

PILE UP ZONE: Great ideas, goals, projects, apps or people to follow up on later

5 PERFORMANCE PILLARS	Give yourself a score of 1-5, 1=low and 5=high in terms of productivity					What could you do to get 1 point higher?
Mental Focus	1	2	3	4	5	
Mental/Emotional/Attitude	1	2	3	4	5	
Productivity	1	2	3	4	5	
Energy	1	2	3	4	5	
Social Connections	1	2	3	4	5	

Win tomorrow today: Plan your top 3 priorities the night before or early in the morning. For each activity, ask yourself "Is there a smarter way to achieve the same outcome?

"There's a tendency to mistake preparation for productivity. You can prepare all you want, but if you never roll the dice you'll never be successful." --Shia LaBeouf

DAY: DAILY THEME:

Win the Day Planning	⭕ **Morning Routine**　　　⭕ **Workday Startup Routine**

Today, I am grateful I get to be a coach because:

I have reviewed my team, recruiting, administrative & personal goals ☐

Today's Results List: List in priority order the top 3 things you can accomplish that would make a measurable impact on your goals and projects? What metric are you trying to hit? Schedule it.

Priority #1:   Metric I am aiming for_____

Priority #2:   Metric I am aiming for_____

Priority #3:   Metric I am aiming for_____

TIME	DAILY SCHEDULE
5 am	
6 am	
7 am	
8 am	
9 am	
10 am	
11 am	
12 pm	
1 pm	
2 pm	
3 pm	
4 pm	
5 pm	
6 pm	
7 pm	
8 pm	
9 pm	
10 pm	
11 pm	

⭕ **Workday Shutdown Routine**　　　⭕ **Evening Routine**

Person/People I need to Lead or Connect with Today (and How to Do It Well)

Staff meeting topics to cover:

What or Who Am I Waiting On To Get a Project Done:

Team meeting topics to cover:

Who Needs Something From Me Today or This Week That I Can Proactively Get To Them?

THE DAILY TO-DO'S

Recruiting:

Calls/texts to make:

On Campus Visits:

Events to Recruit at:

| | Time Spent today |

Team:

| | Time Spent today |

Administrative

| | Time Spent today |

Social Media:

| | Time Spent today |

Personal:

| | Time Spent today |

PILE UP ZONE: Great ideas, goals, projects, apps or people to follow up on later

5 PERFORMANCE PILLARS	Give yourself a score of 1-5, 1=low and 5=high in terms of productivity					What could you do to get 1 point higher?
Mental Focus	1	2	3	4	5	
Mental/Emotional/Attitude	1	2	3	4	5	
Productivity	1	2	3	4	5	
Energy	1	2	3	4	5	
Social Connections	1	2	3	4	5	

Win tomorrow today: Plan your top 3 priorities the night before or early in the morning. For each activity, ask yourself "Is there a smarter way to achieve the same outcome?"

"You only have to do a very few things right in your life so long as you don't do too many things wrong." --Warren Buffett

DAY: _____   DAILY THEME: _____

Win the Day Planning

Today, I am grateful I get to be a coach because:

I have reviewed my team, recruiting, administrative & personal goals ☐

Today's Results List: List in priority order the top 3 things you can accomplish that would make a measurable impact on your goals and projects? What metric are you trying to hit? Schedule it.

Priority #1:   **Metric I am aiming for_____**

Priority #2:   **Metric I am aiming for_____**

Priority #3:   **Metric I am aiming for_____**

○ **Morning Routine**   ○ **Workday Startup Routine**

TIME	DAILY SCHEDULE
5 am	
6 am	
7 am	
8 am	
9 am	
10 am	
11 am	
12 pm	
1 pm	
2 pm	
3 pm	
4 pm	
5 pm	
6 pm	
7 pm	
8 pm	
9 pm	
10 pm	
11 pm	

○ **Workday Shutdown Routine**   ○ **Evening Routine**

Person/People I need to Lead or Connect with Today (and How to Do It Well)

Staff meeting topics to cover:

What or Who Am I Waiting On To Get a Project Done:

Team meeting topics to cover:

Who Needs Something From Me Today or This Week That I Can Proactively Get To Them?

THE DAILY TO-DO'S

Recruiting:

Calls/texts to make:

On Campus Visits:

Events to Recruit at:

Time Spent today

Team:

Time Spent today

Administrative

Time Spent today

Social Media:

Time Spent today

Personal:

Time Spent today

PILE UP ZONE: Great ideas, goals, projects, apps or people to follow up on later

5 PERFORMANCE PILLARS	Give yourself a score of 1-5. 1=low and 5=high in terms of productivity					What could you do to get 1 point higher?
Mental Focus	1	2	3	4	5	
Mental/Emotional/Attitude	1	2	3	4	5	
Productivity	1	2	3	4	5	
Energy	1	2	3	4	5	
Social Connections	1	2	3	4	5	

Win tomorrow today: Plan your top 3 priorities the night before or early in the morning. For each activity, ask yourself "Is there a smarter way to achieve the same outcome?

"When you have to make a choice and don't make it, that in itself is a choice." --William James

DAY: DAILY THEME:

Win the Day Planning		

Today, I am grateful I get to be a coach because:

I have reviewed my team, recruiting, administrative & personal goals ☐

Today's Results List: List in priority order the top 3 things you can accomplish that would make a measurable impact on your goals and projects? What metric are you trying to hit? Schedule it.

Priority #1:   Metric I am aiming for_____

Priority #2:   Metric I am aiming for_____

Priority #3:   Metric I am aiming for_____

○ **Morning Routine**   ○ **Workday Startup Routine**

TIME	DAILY SCHEDULE
5 am	
6 am	
7 am	
8 am	
9 am	
10 am	
11 am	
12 pm	
1 pm	
2 pm	
3 pm	
4 pm	
5 pm	
6 pm	
7 pm	
8 pm	
9 pm	
10 pm	
11 pm	

○ **Workday Shutdown Routine**   ○ **Evening Routine**

Person/People I need to Lead or Connect with Today (and How to Do It Well)

Staff meeting topics to cover:

What or Who Am I Waiting On To Get a Project Done:

Team meeting topics to cover:

Who Needs Something From Me Today or This Week That I Can Proactively Get To Them?

THE DAILY TO-DO'S

Recruiting:

Calls/texts to make:

On Campus Visits:

Events to Recruit at:

Time Spent today

Team:

Time Spent today

Administrative

Time Spent today

Social Media:

Time Spent today

Personal:

Time Spent today

PILE UP ZONE: Great ideas, goals, projects, apps or people to follow up on later

5 PERFORMANCE PILLARS	Give yourself a score of 1-5, 1=low and 5=high in terms of productivity					What could you do to get 1 point higher?
Mental Focus	1	2	3	4	5	
Mental/Emotional/Attitude	1	2	3	4	5	
Productivity	1	2	3	4	5	
Energy	1	2	3	4	5	
Social Connections	1	2	3	4	5	

Win tomorrow today: Plan your top 3 priorities the night before or early in the morning. For each activity, ask yourself "Is there a smarter way to achieve the same outcome?

"Effective performance is preceded by painstaking preparation" --Brian Tracy

DAY: DAILY THEME:

Win the Day Planning

Today, I am grateful I get to be a coach because:

I have reviewed my team, recruiting, administrative & personal goals ☐

Today's Results List: List in priority order the top 3 things you can accomplish that would make a measurable impact on your goals and projects? What metric are you trying to hit? Schedule it.

Priority #1:   Metric I am aiming for_____

Priority #2:   Metric I am aiming for_____

Priority #3:   Metric I am aiming for_____

Person/People I need to Lead or Connect with Today (and How to Do It Well)

What or Who Am I Waiting On To Get a Project Done:

Who Needs Something From Me Today or This Week That I Can Proactively Get To Them?

○ **Morning Routine**   ○ **Workday Startup Routine**

TIME	DAILY SCHEDULE
5 am	
6 am	
7 am	
8 am	
9 am	
10 am	
11 am	
12 pm	
1 pm	
2 pm	
3 pm	
4 pm	
5 pm	
6 pm	
7 pm	
8 pm	
9 pm	
10 pm	
11 pm	

○ **Workday Shutdown Routine**   ○ **Evening Routine**

Staff meeting topics to cover:

Team meeting topics to cover:

THE DAILY TO-DO'S

Recruiting:	Administrative
Calls/texts to make:	
	Time Spent today
On Campus Visits:	Social Media:
Events to Recruit at:	
Time Spent today	Time Spent today
Team:	Personal:
Time Spent today	Time Spent today

PILE UP ZONE: Great ideas, goals, projects, apps or people to follow up on later

5 PERFORMANCE PILLARS	Give yourself a score of 1-5, 1=low and 5=high in terms of productivity					What could you do to get 1 point higher?
Mental Focus	1	2	3	4	5	
Mental/Emotional/Attitude	1	2	3	4	5	
Productivity	1	2	3	4	5	
Energy	1	2	3	4	5	
Social Connections	1	2	3	4	5	

Win tomorrow today: Plan your top 3 priorities the night before or early in the morning. For each activity, ask yourself "Is there a smarter way to achieve the same outcome?"

"You were born to win, but to be a winner, you must plan to win, prepare to win, and expect to win." --Zig Ziglar

DAY: DAILY THEME:

Win the Day Planning

Today, I am grateful I get to be a coach because:

I have reviewed my team, recruiting, administrative & personal goals ☐

Today's Results List: List in priority order the top 3 things you can accomplish that would make a measurable impact on your goals and projects? What metric are you trying to hit? Schedule it.

Priority #1:   **Metric I am aiming for_____**

Priority #2:   **Metric I am aiming for_____**

Priority #3:   **Metric I am aiming for_____**

Person/People I need to Lead or Connect with Today (and How to Do It Well)

What or Who Am I Waiting On To Get a Project Done:

Who Needs Something From Me Today or This Week That I Can Proactively Get To Them?

○ **Morning Routine**   ○ **Workday Startup Routine**

TIME	DAILY SCHEDULE
5 am	
6 am	
7 am	
8 am	
9 am	
10 am	
11 am	
12 pm	
1 pm	
2 pm	
3 pm	
4 pm	
5 pm	
6 pm	
7 pm	
8 pm	
9 pm	
10 pm	
11 pm	

○ **Workday Shutdown Routine**   ○ **Evening Routine**

Staff meeting topics to cover:

Team meeting topics to cover:

THE DAILY TO-DO'S

Recruiting:

Calls/texts to make:

On Campus Visits:

Events to Recruit at:

Time Spent today

Administrative

Time Spent today

Social Media:

Time Spent today

Team:

Time Spent today

Personal:

Time Spent today

PILE UP ZONE: Great ideas, goals, projects, apps or people to follow up on later

5 PERFORMANCE PILLARS	Give yourself a score of 1-5, 1=low and 5=high in terms of productivity					What could you do to get 1 point higher?
Mental Focus	1	2	3	4	5	
Mental/Emotional/Attitude	1	2	3	4	5	
Productivity	1	2	3	4	5	
Energy	1	2	3	4	5	
Social Connections	1	2	3	4	5	

Win tomorrow today: Plan your top 3 priorities the night before or early in the morning. For each activity, ask yourself "Is there a smarter way to achieve the same outcome?"

"Sometimes, things may not go your way, but the effort should be there every single night." --Michael Jordan

DAY: DAILY THEME:

Win the Day Planning

Today, I am grateful I get to be a coach because:

I have reviewed my team, recruiting, administrative & personal goals ☐

Today's Results List: List in priority order the top 3 things you can accomplish that would make a measurable impact on your goals and projects? What metric are you trying to hit? Schedule it.

Priority #1:   Metric I am aiming for_____

Priority #2:   Metric I am aiming for_____

Priority #3:   Metric I am aiming for_____

○ **Morning Routine**   ○ **Workday Startup Routine**

TIME	DAILY SCHEDULE
5 am	
6 am	
7 am	
8 am	
9 am	
10 am	
11 am	
12 pm	
1 pm	
2 pm	
3 pm	
4 pm	
5 pm	
6 pm	
7 pm	
8 pm	
9 pm	
10 pm	
11 pm	

○ **Workday Shutdown Routine**   ○ **Evening Routine**

Person/People I need to Lead or Connect with Today (and How to Do It Well)

Staff meeting topics to cover:

What or Who Am I Waiting On To Get a Project Done:

Team meeting topics to cover:

Who Needs Something From Me Today or This Week That I Can Proactively Get To Them?

THE DAILY TO-DO'S

Recruiting:

Administrative

Calls/texts to make:

| | Time Spent today |

On Campus Visits:

Social Media:

Events to Recruit at:

| Time Spent today | | Time Spent today |

Team:

Personal:

| Time Spent today | | Time Spent today |

PILE UP ZONE: Great ideas, goals, projects, apps or people to follow up on later

5 PERFORMANCE PILLARS	Give yourself a score of 1-5, 1=low and 5=high in terms of productivity					What could you do to get 1 point higher?
Mental Focus	1	2	3	4	5	
Mental/Emotional/Attitude	1	2	3	4	5	
Productivity	1	2	3	4	5	
Energy	1	2	3	4	5	
Social Connections	1	2	3	4	5	

Win tomorrow today: Plan your top 3 priorities the night before or early in the morning.   For each activity, ask yourself "Is there a smarter way to achieve the same outcome?"

"Plans are nothing; planning is everything." --Dwight D. Eisenhower

DAY: _____   DAILY THEME: _____

Win the Day Planning

Today, I am grateful I get to be a coach because:

I have reviewed my team, recruiting, administrative & personal goals ☐

Today's Results List: List in priority order the top 3 things you can accomplish that would make a measurable impact on your goals and projects? What metric are you trying to hit? Schedule it.

Priority #1:   **Metric I am aiming for_____**

Priority #2:   **Metric I am aiming for_____**

Priority #3:   **Metric I am aiming for_____**

○ **Morning Routine**   ○ **Workday Startup Routine**

TIME	DAILY SCHEDULE
5 am	
6 am	
7 am	
8 am	
9 am	
10 am	
11 am	
12 pm	
1 pm	
2 pm	
3 pm	
4 pm	
5 pm	
6 pm	
7 pm	
8 pm	
9 pm	
10 pm	
11 pm	

○ **Workday Shutdown Routine**   ○ **Evening Routine**

Person/People I need to Lead or Connect with Today (and How to Do It Well)

Staff meeting topics to cover:

What or Who Am I Waiting On To Get a Project Done:

Team meeting topics to cover:

Who Needs Something From Me Today or This Week That I Can Proactively Get To Them?

THE DAILY TO-DO'S

Recruiting:

Calls/texts to make:

On Campus Visits:

Events to Recruit at:

Time Spent today

Administrative

Time Spent today

Social Media:

Time Spent today

Team:

Time Spent today

Personal:

Time Spent today

PILE UP ZONE: Great ideas, goals, projects, apps or people to follow up on later

5 PERFORMANCE PILLARS	Give yourself a score of 1-5, 1=low and 5=high in terms of productivity					What could you do to get 1 point higher?
Mental Focus	1	2	3	4	5	
Mental/Emotional/Attitude	1	2	3	4	5	
Productivity	1	2	3	4	5	
Energy	1	2	3	4	5	
Social Connections	1	2	3	4	5	

Win tomorrow today: Plan your top 3 priorities the night before or early in the morning.   For each activity, ask yourself "Is there a smarter way to achieve the same outcome?

"There are risks and costs to action. But they are far less than the long-range risks of comfortable inaction."
-John F. Kennedy

DAY: DAILY THEME:

Win the Day Planning

Today, I am grateful I get to be a coach because:

I have reviewed my team, recruiting, administrative & personal goals ☐

Today's Results List: List in priority order the top 3 things you can accomplish that would make a measurable impact on your goals and projects? What metric are you trying to hit? Schedule it.

Priority #1:   Metric I am aiming for_____

Priority #2:   Metric I am aiming for_____

Priority #3:   Metric I am aiming for_____

Person/People I need to Lead or Connect with Today (and How to Do It Well)

What or Who Am I Waiting On To Get a Project Done:

Who Needs Something From Me Today or This Week That I Can Proactively Get To Them?

○ **Morning Routine**   ○ **Workday Startup Routine**

TIME	DAILY SCHEDULE
5 am	
6 am	
7 am	
8 am	
9 am	
10 am	
11 am	
12 pm	
1 pm	
2 pm	
3 pm	
4 pm	
5 pm	
6 pm	
7 pm	
8 pm	
9 pm	
10 pm	
11 pm	

○ **Workday Shutdown Routine**   ○ **Evening Routine**

Staff meeting topics to cover:

Team meeting topics to cover:

THE DAILY TO-DO'S

Recruiting:

Administrative

Calls/texts to make:

Time Spent today

On Campus Visits:

Social Media:

Events to Recruit at:

Time Spent today

Time Spent today

Team:

Personal:

Time Spent today

Time Spent today

PILE UP ZONE: Great ideas, goals, projects, apps or people to follow up on later

5 PERFORMANCE PILLARS	Give yourself a score of 1-5, 1=low and 5=high in terms of productivity					What could you do to get 1 point higher?
Mental Focus	1	2	3	4	5	
Mental/Emotional/Attitude	1	2	3	4	5	
Productivity	1	2	3	4	5	
Energy	1	2	3	4	5	
Social Connections	1	2	3	4	5	

Win tomorrow today: Plan your top 3 priorities the night before or early in the morning. For each activity, ask yourself "Is there a smarter way to achieve the same outcome?

"The simple act of paying positive attention to people has a great deal to do with productivity." --Tom Peters

DAY: DAILY THEME:

Win the Day Planning

Today, I am grateful I get to be a coach because:

I have reviewed my team, recruiting, administrative & personal goals ☐

Today's Results List: List in priority order the top 3 things you can accomplish that would make a measurable impact on your goals and projects? What metric are you trying to hit? Schedule it.

Priority #1:   **Metric I am aiming for_____**

Priority #2:   **Metric I am aiming for_____**

Priority #3:   **Metric I am aiming for_____**

○ **Morning Routine**   ○ **Workday Startup Routine**

TIME	DAILY SCHEDULE
5 am	
6 am	
7 am	
8 am	
9 am	
10 am	
11 am	
12 pm	
1 pm	
2 pm	
3 pm	
4 pm	
5 pm	
6 pm	
7 pm	
8 pm	
9 pm	
10 pm	
11 pm	

○ **Workday Shutdown Routine**   ○ **Evening Routine**

Person/People I need to Lead or Connect with Today (and How to Do It Well)

Staff meeting topics to cover:

What or Who Am I Waiting On To Get a Project Done:

Team meeting topics to cover:

Who Needs Something From Me Today or This Week That I Can Proactively Get To Them?

THE DAILY TO-DO'S

Recruiting:

Calls/texts to make:

On Campus Visits:

Events to Recruit at:

Time Spent today

Team:

Time Spent today

Administrative

Time Spent today

Social Media:

Time Spent today

Personal:

Time Spent today

PILE UP ZONE: Great ideas, goals, projects, apps or people to follow up on later

5 PERFORMANCE PILLARS	Give yourself a score of 1-5, 1=low and 5=high in terms of productivity					What could you do to get 1 point higher?
Mental Focus	1	2	3	4	5	
Mental/Emotional/Attitude	1	2	3	4	5	
Productivity	1	2	3	4	5	
Energy	1	2	3	4	5	
Social Connections	1	2	3	4	5	

Win tomorrow today: Plan your top 3 priorities the night before or early in the morning. For each activity, ask yourself "Is there a smarter way to achieve the same outcome?

"Amateurs sit and wait for inspiration, the rest of us just get up and go to work." --Stephen King

DAY: DAILY THEME:

Win the Day Planning

Today, I am grateful I get to be a coach because:

I have reviewed my team, recruiting, administrative & personal goals ☐

Today's Results List: List in priority order the top 3 things you can accomplish that would make a measurable impact on your goals and projects? What metric are you trying to hit? Schedule it.

Priority #1:   Metric I am aiming for_____

Priority #2:   Metric I am aiming for_____

Priority #3:   Metric I am aiming for_____

Person/People I need to Lead or Connect with Today (and How to Do It Well)

What or Who Am I Waiting On To Get a Project Done:

Who Needs Something From Me Today or This Week That I Can Proactively Get To Them?

○ **Morning Routine**   ○ **Workday Startup Routine**

TIME	DAILY SCHEDULE
5 am	
6 am	
7 am	
8 am	
9 am	
10 am	
11 am	
12 pm	
1 pm	
2 pm	
3 pm	
4 pm	
5 pm	
6 pm	
7 pm	
8 pm	
9 pm	
10 pm	
11 pm	

○ **Workday Shutdown Routine**   ○ **Evening Routine**

Staff meeting topics to cover:

Team meeting topics to cover:

THE DAILY TO-DO'S

Recruiting:

Calls/texts to make:

On Campus Visits:

Events to Recruit at:

Time Spent today

Team:

Time Spent today

Administrative

Time Spent today

Social Media:

Time Spent today

Personal:

Time Spent today

PILE UP ZONE: Great ideas, goals, projects, apps or people to follow up on later

5 PERFORMANCE PILLARS	Give yourself a score of 1-5, 1=low and 5=high in terms of productivity					What could you do to get 1 point higher?
Mental Focus	1	2	3	4	5	
Mental/Emotional/Attitude	1	2	3	4	5	
Productivity	1	2	3	4	5	
Energy	1	2	3	4	5	
Social Connections	1	2	3	4	5	

Win tomorrow today: Plan your top 3 priorities the night before or early in the morning. For each activity, ask yourself "Is there a smarter way to achieve the same outcome?"

"Whenever you are asked if you can do a job, tell 'em, 'Certainly I can!' Then get busy and find out how to do it."
--Theodore Roosevelt

DAY: _____   DAILY THEME: _____

Win the Day Planning

Today, I am grateful I get to be a coach because:

I have reviewed my team, recruiting, administrative & personal goals ☐

Today's Results List: List in priority order the top 3 things you can accomplish that would make a measurable impact on your goals and projects? What metric are you trying to hit? Schedule it.

Priority #1:   Metric I am aiming for_____

Priority #2:   Metric I am aiming for_____

Priority #3:   Metric I am aiming for_____

○ **Morning Routine**   ○ **Workday Startup Routine**

TIME	DAILY SCHEDULE
5 am	
6 am	
7 am	
8 am	
9 am	
10 am	
11 am	
12 pm	
1 pm	
2 pm	
3 pm	
4 pm	
5 pm	
6 pm	
7 pm	
8 pm	
9 pm	
10 pm	
11 pm	

○ **Workday Shutdown Routine**   ○ **Evening Routine**

Person/People I need to Lead or Connect with Today (and How to Do It Well)

Staff meeting topics to cover:

What or Who Am I Waiting On To Get a Project Done:

Team meeting topics to cover:

Who Needs Something From Me Today or This Week That I Can Proactively Get To Them?

THE DAILY TO-DO'S

Recruiting:

Calls/texts to make:

On Campus Visits:

Events to Recruit at:

Time Spent today

Team:

Time Spent today

Administrative

Time Spent today

Social Media:

Time Spent today

Personal:

Time Spent today

PILE UP ZONE: Great ideas, goals, projects, apps or people to follow up on later

5 PERFORMANCE PILLARS	Give yourself a score of 1-5, 1=low and 5=high in terms of productivity					What could you do to get 1 point higher?
Mental Focus	1	2	3	4	5	
Mental/Emotional/Attitude	1	2	3	4	5	
Productivity	1	2	3	4	5	
Energy	1	2	3	4	5	
Social Connections	1	2	3	4	5	

Win tomorrow today: Plan your top 3 priorities the night before or early in the morning. For each activity, ask yourself "Is there a smarter way to achieve the same outcome?"

"Time is an equal opportunity employer. Each human being has exactly the same number of hours and minutes in a day." -- Denis Waitley

DAY: DAILY THEME:

Win the Day Planning

Today, I am grateful I get to be a coach because:

I have reviewed my team, recruiting, administrative & personal goals ☐

Today's Results List: List in priority order the top 3 things you can accomplish that would make a measurable impact on your goals and projects? What metric are you trying to hit? Schedule it.

Priority #1:   **Metric I am aiming for_____**

Priority #2:   **Metric I am aiming for_____**

Priority #3:   **Metric I am aiming for_____**

Person/People I need to Lead or Connect with Today (and How to Do It Well)

What or Who Am I Waiting On To Get a Project Done:

Who Needs Something From Me Today or This Week That I Can Proactively Get To Them?

○ **Morning Routine**   ○ **Workday Startup Routine**

TIME	DAILY SCHEDULE
5 am	
6 am	
7 am	
8 am	
9 am	
10 am	
11 am	
12 pm	
1 pm	
2 pm	
3 pm	
4 pm	
5 pm	
6 pm	
7 pm	
8 pm	
9 pm	
10 pm	
11 pm	

○ **Workday Shutdown Routine**   ○ **Evening Routine**

Staff meeting topics to cover:

Team meeting topics to cover:

THE DAILY TO-DO'S

Recruiting:

Calls/texts to make:

On Campus Visits:

Events to Recruit at:

Time Spent today

Team:

Time Spent today

Administrative

Time Spent today

Social Media:

Time Spent today

Personal:

Time Spent today

PILE UP ZONE: Great ideas, goals, projects, apps or people to follow up on later

5 PERFORMANCE PILLARS	Give yourself a score of 1-5. 1=low and 5=high in terms of productivity					What could you do to get 1 point higher?
Mental Focus	1	2	3	4	5	
Mental/Emotional/Attitude	1	2	3	4	5	
Productivity	1	2	3	4	5	
Energy	1	2	3	4	5	
Social Connections	1	2	3	4	5	

Win tomorrow today: Plan your top 3 priorities the night before or early in the morning. For each activity, ask yourself "Is there a smarter way to achieve the same outcome?

"He who is not courageous enough to take risks will accomplish nothing in life." --Muhammad Ali

DAY: DAILY THEME:

Win the Day Planning

Today, I am grateful I get to be a coach because:

I have reviewed my team, recruiting, administrative & personal goals ☐

Today's Results List: List in priority order the top 3 things you can accomplish that would make a measurable impact on your goals and projects? What metric are you trying to hit? Schedule it.

Priority #1:   Metric I am aiming for_____

Priority #2:   Metric I am aiming for_____

Priority #3:   Metric I am aiming for_____

Person/People I need to Lead or Connect with Today (and How to Do It Well)

What or Who Am I Waiting On To Get a Project Done:

Who Needs Something From Me Today or This Week That I Can Proactively Get To Them?

O **Morning Routine**   O **Workday Startup Routine**

TIME	DAILY SCHEDULE
5 am	
6 am	
7 am	
8 am	
9 am	
10 am	
11 am	
12 pm	
1 pm	
2 pm	
3 pm	
4 pm	
5 pm	
6 pm	
7 pm	
8 pm	
9 pm	
10 pm	
11 pm	

O **Workday Shutdown Routine**   O **Evening Routine**

Staff meeting topics to cover:

Team meeting topics to cover:

THE DAILY TO-DO'S

Recruiting:

Calls/texts to make:

On Campus Visits:

Events to Recruit at:

Time Spent today

Administrative

Time Spent today

Social Media:

Time Spent today

Team:

Time Spent today

Personal:

Time Spent today

PILE UP ZONE: Great ideas, goals, projects, apps or people to follow up on later

5 PERFORMANCE PILLARS	Give yourself a score of 1-5, 1=low and 5=high in terms of productivity					What could you do to get 1 point higher?
Mental Focus	1	2	3	4	5	
Mental/Emotional/Attitude	1	2	3	4	5	
Productivity	1	2	3	4	5	
Energy	1	2	3	4	5	
Social Connections	1	2	3	4	5	

Win tomorrow today: Plan your top 3 priorities the night before or early in the morning. For each activity, ask yourself "Is there a smarter way to achieve the same outcome?

"Tomorrow hopes we have learned something from yesterday." --John Wayne

DAY: DAILY THEME:

Win the Day Planning

Today, I am grateful I get to be a coach because:

I have reviewed my team, recruiting, administrative & personal goals ☐

Today's Results List: List in priority order the top 3 things you can accomplish that would make a measurable impact on your goals and projects? What metric are you trying to hit? Schedule it.

Priority #1:   Metric I am aiming for_____

Priority #2:   Metric I am aiming for_____

Priority #3:   Metric I am aiming for_____

○ **Morning Routine**   ○ **Workday Startup Routine**

TIME	DAILY SCHEDULE
5 am	
6 am	
7 am	
8 am	
9 am	
10 am	
11 am	
12 pm	
1 pm	
2 pm	
3 pm	
4 pm	
5 pm	
6 pm	
7 pm	
8 pm	
9 pm	
10 pm	
11 pm	

○ **Workday Shutdown Routine**   ○ **Evening Routine**

Person/People I need to Lead or Connect with Today (and How to Do It Well)

What or Who Am I Waiting On To Get a Project Done:

Who Needs Something From Me Today or This Week That I Can Proactively Get To Them?

Staff meeting topics to cover:

Team meeting topics to cover:

THE DAILY TO-DO'S

Recruiting:	Administrative
Calls/texts to make:	
	Time Spent today
On Campus Visits:	Social Media:
Events to Recruit at:	
	Time Spent today
	Time Spent today
Team:	Personal:
	Time Spent today
	Time Spent today

PILE UP ZONE: Great ideas, goals, projects, apps or people to follow up on later

5 PERFORMANCE PILLARS	Give yourself a score of 1-5, 1=low and 5=high in terms of productivity					What could you do to get 1 point higher?
Mental Focus	1	2	3	4	5	
Mental/Emotional/Attitude	1	2	3	4	5	
Productivity	1	2	3	4	5	
Energy	1	2	3	4	5	
Social Connections	1	2	3	4	5	

Win tomorrow today: Plan your top 3 priorities the night before or early in the morning. For each activity, ask yourself "Is there a smarter way to achieve the same outcome?

"Don't watch the clock; do what it does. Keep going." --Sam Levenson

DAY: _____   DAILY THEME: _____

Win the Day Planning

Today, I am grateful I get to be a coach because:

I have reviewed my team, recruiting, administrative & personal goals ☐

Today's Results List: List in priority order the top 3 things you can accomplish that would make a measurable impact on your goals and projects? What metric are you trying to hit? Schedule it.

Priority #1:   Metric I am aiming for_____

Priority #2:   Metric I am aiming for_____

Priority #3:   Metric I am aiming for_____

Person/People I need to Lead or Connect with Today (and How to Do It Well)

What or Who Am I Waiting On To Get a Project Done:

Who Needs Something From Me Today or This Week That I Can Proactively Get To Them?

○ **Morning Routine**   ○ **Workday Startup Routine**

TIME	DAILY SCHEDULE
5 am	
6 am	
7 am	
8 am	
9 am	
10 am	
11 am	
12 pm	
1 pm	
2 pm	
3 pm	
4 pm	
5 pm	
6 pm	
7 pm	
8 pm	
9 pm	
10 pm	
11 pm	

○ **Workday Shutdown Routine**   ○ **Evening Routine**

Staff meeting topics to cover:

Team meeting topics to cover:

THE DAILY TO-DO'S

Recruiting:

Calls/texts to make:

On Campus Visits:

Events to Recruit at:

Time Spent today

Administrative

Time Spent today

Social Media:

Time Spent today

Team:

Time Spent today

Personal:

Time Spent today

PILE UP ZONE: Great ideas, goals, projects, apps or people to follow up on later

5 PERFORMANCE PILLARS	Give yourself a score of 1-5, 1=low and 5=high in terms of productivity					What could you do to get 1 point higher?
Mental Focus	1	2	3	4	5	
Mental/Emotional/Attitude	1	2	3	4	5	
Productivity	1	2	3	4	5	
Energy	1	2	3	4	5	
Social Connections	1	2	3	4	5	

Win tomorrow today: Plan your top 3 priorities the night before or early in the morning. For each activity, ask yourself "Is there a smarter way to achieve the same outcome?

"Take time to deliberate, but when the time for action has arrived, stop thinking and go in." -- Napoleon Bonaparte

DAY: _____   DAILY THEME: _____

Win the Day Planning

Today, I am grateful I get to be a coach because:

I have reviewed my team, recruiting, administrative & personal goals ☐

Today's Results List: List in priority order the top 3 things you can accomplish that would make a measurable impact on your goals and projects? What metric are you trying to hit? Schedule it.

Priority #1:   **Metric I am aiming for_____**

Priority #2:   **Metric I am aiming for_____**

Priority #3:   **Metric I am aiming for_____**

Person/People I need to Lead or Connect with Today (and How to Do It Well)

What or Who Am I Waiting On To Get a Project Done:

Who Needs Something From Me Today or This Week That I Can Proactively Get To Them?

○ **Morning Routine**   ○ **Workday Startup Routine**

TIME	DAILY SCHEDULE
5 am	
6 am	
7 am	
8 am	
9 am	
10 am	
11 am	
12 pm	
1 pm	
2 pm	
3 pm	
4 pm	
5 pm	
6 pm	
7 pm	
8 pm	
9 pm	
10 pm	
11 pm	

○ **Workday Shutdown Routine**   ○ **Evening Routine**

Staff meeting topics to cover:

Team meeting topics to cover:

THE DAILY TO-DO'S

Recruiting:

Administrative

Calls/texts to make:

Time Spent today

On Campus Visits:

Social Media:

Events to Recruit at:

Time Spent today

Time Spent today

Team:

Personal:

Time Spent today

Time Spent today

PILE UP ZONE: Great ideas, goals, projects, apps or people to follow up on later

5 PERFORMANCE PILLARS	Give yourself a score of 1-5, 1=low and 5=high in terms of productivity					What could you do to get 1 point higher?
Mental Focus	1	2	3	4	5	
Mental/Emotional/Attitude	1	2	3	4	5	
Productivity	1	2	3	4	5	
Energy	1	2	3	4	5	
Social Connections	1	2	3	4	5	

Win tomorrow today: Plan your top 3 priorities the night before or early in the morning. For each activity, ask yourself "Is there a smarter way to achieve the same outcome?"

"What looks like multitasking is really switching back and forth between multiple tasks, which reduces productivity and increases mistakes by up to 50 percent." --Susan Cain

4 WEEK - PLAN, DO, REVIEW, AND IMPROVE THE SYSTEM

Here is your chance to reflect back on the last month and see...

What should I/we stop doing? What should I/we do less? What should I/we continue doing? What should I/we do more? What should I/we start doing?

Reflect back on your activities to track and see your progress, notice patterns and review your accomplishments, gives you the opportunity to adjust, re-invent and plan your next 4 weeks.

The cycle is: Do the work → Look back → Look forward → Plan the next 4 weeks → Do the work...

	What Should I/We Stop Doing?	What Should I/We Do Less?	What Should I/We Continue Doing?	What Should I/we Do More Of?	What Should I/We Start Doing?
Recruiting Goals, Processes, Daily Activities					
Team Goals, Projects, Daily Activities					
Administrative Goals, Projects, Daily Activities					
Personal Goals, Projects, Daily Activities					
5 Performance Pillars					

4 WEEK SPRINT - PLAN, DO, REVIEW, AND IMPROVE THE SYSTEM

TIME AUDIT:

	Actual Time Spent	Ideal Time Spent	Adjustments to make:
Recruiting			
Team			
Administrative			
Social Media			
Personal			

3 big wins over the last 30 days were . . .

My biggest struggle over the last 30 days was. . .

. .and if I were advising or mentoring someone dealing with the same struggle, I'd advise them to . . .

4 WEEK PERFORMANCE REVIEW

Score yourself on a scale of 1 to 5 in each of the areas below, with 5 being the best. Also, write any notes in the bubbles about what is happening in that area or what you would like to improve. Be honest, but also be kind to yourself. Tally your scores up and multiply by 2, and that will give you a score out of 100. Basically, you're doing a spot check on your life and giving yourself a score so that you know where you are.

RECRUITING	ADMINISTRATIVE	TEAM/STAFF	SOCIAL MEDIA	PRODUCTIVITY
Score 1-5_____	Score 1-5_____	Score 1-5_____	Score 1-5_____	Score 1-5_____

HEALTH/ENERGY	MENTAL/EMOTIONAL	FAMILY	FRIENDS	FOCUS
Score 1-5_____	Score 1-5_____	Score 1-5_____	Score 1-5_____	Score 1-5_____

MONTH / YEAR: THEME:

		SUNDAY	MONDAY	TUESDAY

FOCUS AREAS FOR GROWTH AND IMPROVEMENT THIS MONTH

1.

2.

3.

STRATEGIES/PROJECTS TO HELP REACH GOALS

Establish 1-2 projects that are going to help you reach the goals you listed above.

Major Events
Write down any major events coming up this month, and how you can prepare for them.

These things MUST happen this month

How do you build your program exponentially in a relatively short amount of time? Through focus. Use this section in each area to drive the direction of your month, week, and day to eliminate activities that just do NOT fit in. Always refer back to your focus and ask yourself..."Am I working on things that support my focus?", etc.

WEDNESDAY	THURSDAY	FRIDAY	SATURDAY

Recruiting deadlines/outcomes we need this month Include:	The best ways I can prepare and ensure that I show up to win this month are:

YOUR IDEAL WEEK

FOCUS AREA FOR GROWTH AND IM-PROVEMENT THIS WEEK	✓
1.	○
2.	○
3.	○

Focus Areas

TIME	MONDAY	TUESDAY	WEDNESDAY
5:00 - 5:30 AM			
6:00 - 6:30 AM			
7:00 - 7:30 AM			
8:00 - 8:30 AM			
9:00 - 9:30 AM			
10:00 - 10:30 AM			
11:00 - 11:30 AM			
12:00 - 12:30 PM			
1:00 - 1:30 PM			
2:00 - 2:30 PM			
3:00 - 3:30 PM			
4:00 - 4:30 PM			
5:00 - 5:30 PM			
6:00 - 6:30 PM			
7:00 - 7:30 PM			
8:00 - 8:30 PM			
9:00 - 9:30 PM			
10:00 - 10:30 PM			
11:00 - 11:30 PM			
12:00 - 12:30 AM			

HOW TO SCHEDULE YOUR IDEAL WEEK

Make time for what matters first.

Note on this calendar when you will have:

1. Family time
2. Weekly reflection
3. Self-care time
4. Wake up time
5. Go to bed time
6. Work stop time
7. Practice
8. Weights
9. Meetings
10. After all of this is set, what big blocks of time to do you have left for the growth and improvement projects you listed above? Find at least 1 hour each day and block it off.
11. Fit all of the busy work in between your blocks of program building projects.

Last week's wins & lessons learned:

USE THIS PAGE TO CREATE AN OVERVIEW FOR NEXT WEEK

THURSDAY	FRIDAY	SATURDAY	SUNDAY

Thoughts for this upcoming week:

DAY: _____   DAILY THEME: _____

Win the Day Planning

Today, I am grateful I get to be a coach because:

I have reviewed my team, recruiting, administrative & personal goals ☐

Today's Results List: List in priority order the top 3 things you can accomplish that would make a measurable impact on your goals and projects? What metric are you trying to hit? Schedule it.

Priority #1:   Metric I am aiming for_____

Priority #2:   Metric I am aiming for_____

Priority #3:   Metric I am aiming for_____

○ **Morning Routine**   ○ **Workday Startup Routine**

TIME	DAILY SCHEDULE
5 am	
6 am	
7 am	
8 am	
9 am	
10 am	
11 am	
12 pm	
1 pm	
2 pm	
3 pm	
4 pm	
5 pm	
6 pm	
7 pm	
8 pm	
9 pm	
10 pm	
11 pm	

○ **Workday Shutdown Routine**   ○ **Evening Routine**

Person/People I need to Lead or Connect with Today (and How to Do It Well)

Staff meeting topics to cover:

What or Who Am I Waiting On To Get a Project Done:

Team meeting topics to cover:

Who Needs Something From Me Today or This Week That I Can Proactively Get To Them?

THE DAILY TO-DO'S

Recruiting:

Calls/texts to make:

On Campus Visits:

Events to Recruit at:

| Time Spent today |

Team:

| Time Spent today |

Administrative

| Time Spent today |

Social Media:

| Time Spent today |

Personal:

| Time Spent today |

PILE UP ZONE: Great ideas, goals, projects, apps or people to follow up on later

5 PERFORMANCE PILLARS	Give yourself a score of 1-5, 1=low and 5=high in terms of productivity					What could you do to get 1 point higher?
Mental Focus	1	2	3	4	5	
Mental/Emotional/Attitude	1	2	3	4	5	
Productivity	1	2	3	4	5	
Energy	1	2	3	4	5	
Social Connections	1	2	3	4	5	

Win tomorrow today: Plan your top 3 priorities the night before or early in the morning. For each activity, ask yourself "Is there a smarter way to achieve the same outcome?"

"Obstacles are those frightful things you see when you take your eyes off the goal." --Henry Ford

163

DAY: DAILY THEME:

Win the Day Planning

Today, I am grateful I get to be a coach because:

I have reviewed my team, recruiting, administrative & personal goals ☐

Today's Results List: List in priority order the top 3 things you can accomplish that would make a measurable impact on your goals and projects? What metric are you trying to hit? Schedule it.

Priority #1:   **Metric I am aiming for_____**

Priority #2:   **Metric I am aiming for_____**

Priority #3:   **Metric I am aiming for_____**

Person/People I need to Lead or Connect with Today (and How to Do It Well)

What or Who Am I Waiting On To Get a Project Done:

Who Needs Something From Me Today or This Week That I Can Proactively Get To Them?

○ **Morning Routine**   ○ **Workday Startup Routine**

TIME	DAILY SCHEDULE
5 am	
6 am	
7 am	
8 am	
9 am	
10 am	
11 am	
12 pm	
1 pm	
2 pm	
3 pm	
4 pm	
5 pm	
6 pm	
7 pm	
8 pm	
9 pm	
10 pm	
11 pm	

○ **Workday Shutdown Routine**   ○ **Evening Routine**

Staff meeting topics to cover:

Team meeting topics to cover:

THE DAILY TO-DO'S

Recruiting:

Calls/texts to make:

On Campus Visits:

Events to Recruit at:

Time Spent today

Administrative

Time Spent today

Social Media:

Time Spent today

Team:

Time Spent today

Personal:

Time Spent today

PILE UP ZONE: Great ideas, goals, projects, apps or people to follow up on later

5 PERFORMANCE PILLARS	Give yourself a score of 1-5. 1=low and 5=high in terms of productivity					What could you do to get 1 point higher?
Mental Focus	1	2	3	4	5	
Mental/Emotional/Attitude	1	2	3	4	5	
Productivity	1	2	3	4	5	
Energy	1	2	3	4	5	
Social Connections	1	2	3	4	5	

Win tomorrow today: Plan your top 3 priorities the night before or early in the morning. For each activity, ask yourself "Is there a smarter way to achieve the same outcome?

"Over the long run, the unglamorous habit of frequency fosters both productivity and creativity."
--Gretchen Rubin

DAY: DAILY THEME:

Win the Day Planning

Today, I am grateful I get to be a coach because:

I have reviewed my team, recruiting, administrative & personal goals ☐

Today's Results List: List in priority order the top 3 things you can accomplish that would make a measurable impact on your goals and projects? What metric are you trying to hit? Schedule it.

Priority #1:   Metric I am aiming for_____

Priority #2:   Metric I am aiming for_____

Priority #3:   Metric I am aiming for_____

Person/People I need to Lead or Connect with Today (and How to Do It Well)

What or Who Am I Waiting On To Get a Project Done:

Who Needs Something From Me Today or This Week That I Can Proactively Get To Them?

○ **Morning Routine**   ○ **Workday Startup Routine**

TIME	DAILY SCHEDULE
5 am	
6 am	
7 am	
8 am	
9 am	
10 am	
11 am	
12 pm	
1 pm	
2 pm	
3 pm	
4 pm	
5 pm	
6 pm	
7 pm	
8 pm	
9 pm	
10 pm	
11 pm	

○ **Workday Shutdown Routine**   ○ **Evening Routine**

Staff meeting topics to cover:

Team meeting topics to cover:

THE DAILY TO-DO'S

Recruiting:

Administrative

Calls/texts to make:

	Time Spent today

On Campus Visits:

Social Media:

Events to Recruit at:

Time Spent today		Time Spent today

Team:

Personal:

Time Spent today		Time Spent today

PILE UP ZONE: Great ideas, goals, projects, apps or people to follow up on later

5 PERFORMANCE PILLARS	Give yourself a score of 1-5, 1=low and 5=high in terms of productivity					What could you do to get 1 point higher?
Mental Focus	1	2	3	4	5	
Mental/Emotional/Attitude	1	2	3	4	5	
Productivity	1	2	3	4	5	
Energy	1	2	3	4	5	
Social Connections	1	2	3	4	5	

Win tomorrow today: Plan your top 3 priorities the night before or early in the morning. For each activity, ask yourself "Is there a smarter way to achieve the same outcome?"

"Nothing in the world can take the place of persistence." --Calvin Coolidge

DAY: _____   DAILY THEME: _____

Win the Day Planning

Today, I am grateful I get to be a coach because:

I have reviewed my team, recruiting, administrative & personal goals ☐

Today's Results List: List in priority order the top 3 things you can accomplish that would make a measurable impact on your goals and projects? What metric are you trying to hit? Schedule it.

Priority #1:   Metric I am aiming for_____

Priority #2:   Metric I am aiming for_____

Priority #3:   Metric I am aiming for_____

Person/People I need to Lead or Connect with Today (and How to Do It Well)

What or Who Am I Waiting On To Get a Project Done:

Who Needs Something From Me Today or This Week That I Can Proactively Get To Them?

○ **Morning Routine**   ○ **Workday Startup Routine**

TIME	DAILY SCHEDULE
5 am	
6 am	
7 am	
8 am	
9 am	
10 am	
11 am	
12 pm	
1 pm	
2 pm	
3 pm	
4 pm	
5 pm	
6 pm	
7 pm	
8 pm	
9 pm	
10 pm	
11 pm	

○ **Workday Shutdown Routine**   ○ **Evening Routine**

Staff meeting topics to cover:

Team meeting topics to cover:

THE DAILY TO-DO'S

Use this space to capture tasks, notes, or answer the questions: What happened in your day? What did you learn?

Recruiting:

Calls/texts to make:

On Campus Visits:

Events to Recruit at:

Time Spent today

Administrative

Time Spent today

Social Media:

Time Spent today

Team:

Time Spent today

Personal:

Time Spent today

PILE UP ZONE: Great ideas, goals, projects, apps or people to follow up on later

5 PERFORMANCE PILLARS	Give yourself a score of 1-5. 1=low and 5=high in terms of productivity					What could you do to get 1 point higher?
Mental Focus	1	2	3	4	5	
Mental/Emotional/Attitude	1	2	3	4	5	
Productivity	1	2	3	4	5	
Energy	1	2	3	4	5	
Social Connections	1	2	3	4	5	

Win tomorrow today: Plan your top 3 priorities the night before or early in the morning. For each activity, ask yourself "Is there a smarter way to achieve the same outcome?"

"Work hard, have fun, and make history." --Jeff Bezos

DAY: DAILY THEME:

Win the Day Planning

Today, I am grateful I get to be a coach because:

I have reviewed my team, recruiting, administrative & personal goals ☐

Today's Results List: List in priority order the top 3 things you can accomplish that would make a measurable impact on your goals and projects? What metric are you trying to hit? Schedule it.

Priority #1:   **Metric I am aiming for_____**

Priority #2:   **Metric I am aiming for_____**

Priority #3:   **Metric I am aiming for_____**

Person/People I need to Lead or Connect with Today (and How to Do It Well)

What or Who Am I Waiting On To Get a Project Done:

Who Needs Something From Me Today or This Week That I Can Proactively Get To Them?

○ **Morning Routine**   ○ **Workday Startup Routine**

TIME	DAILY SCHEDULE
5 am	
6 am	
7 am	
8 am	
9 am	
10 am	
11 am	
12 pm	
1 pm	
2 pm	
3 pm	
4 pm	
5 pm	
6 pm	
7 pm	
8 pm	
9 pm	
10 pm	
11 pm	

○ **Workday Shutdown Routine**   ○ **Evening Routine**

Staff meeting topics to cover:

Team meeting topics to cover:

THE DAILY TO-DO'S

Recruiting:

Administrative

Calls/texts to make:

Time Spent today

On Campus Visits:

Social Media:

Events to Recruit at:

Time Spent today

Time Spent today

Team:

Personal:

Time Spent today

Time Spent today

PILE UP ZONE: Great ideas, goals, projects, apps or people to follow up on later

5 PERFORMANCE PILLARS	Give yourself a score of 1-5, 1=low and 5=high in terms of productivity					What could you do to get 1 point higher?
Mental Focus	1	2	3	4	5	
Mental/Emotional/Attitude	1	2	3	4	5	
Productivity	1	2	3	4	5	
Energy	1	2	3	4	5	
Social Connections	1	2	3	4	5	

Win tomorrow today: Plan your top 3 priorities the night before or early in the morning.   For each activity, ask yourself "Is there a smarter way to achieve the same outcome?

"If you want something done, give it to a busy man." --Preston Sturges

DAY: DAILY THEME:

Win the Day Planning

Today, I am grateful I get to be a coach because:

I have reviewed my team, recruiting, administrative & personal goals ☐

Today's Results List: List in priority order the top 3 things you can accomplish that would make a measurable impact on your goals and projects? What metric are you trying to hit? Schedule it.

Priority #1:   **Metric I am aiming for_____**

Priority #2:   **Metric I am aiming for_____**

Priority #3:   **Metric I am aiming for_____**

Person/People I need to Lead or Connect with Today (and How to Do It Well)

What or Who Am I Waiting On To Get a Project Done:

Who Needs Something From Me Today or This Week That I Can Proactively Get To Them?

○ **Morning Routine**   ○ **Workday Startup Routine**

TIME	DAILY SCHEDULE
5 am	
6 am	
7 am	
8 am	
9 am	
10 am	
11 am	
12 pm	
1 pm	
2 pm	
3 pm	
4 pm	
5 pm	
6 pm	
7 pm	
8 pm	
9 pm	
10 pm	
11 pm	

○ **Workday Shutdown Routine**   ○ **Evening Routine**

Staff meeting topics to cover:

Team meeting topics to cover:

THE DAILY TO-DO'S

Recruiting:

Calls/texts to make:

On Campus Visits:

Events to Recruit at:

Time Spent today

Team:

Time Spent today

Administrative

Time Spent today

Social Media:

Time Spent today

Personal:

Time Spent today

PILE UP ZONE: Great ideas, goals, projects, apps or people to follow up on later

5 PERFORMANCE PILLARS	Give yourself a score of 1-5, 1=low and 5=high in terms of productivity					What could you do to get 1 point higher?
Mental Focus	1	2	3	4	5	
Mental/Emotional/Attitude	1	2	3	4	5	
Productivity	1	2	3	4	5	
Energy	1	2	3	4	5	
Social Connections	1	2	3	4	5	

Win tomorrow today: Plan your top 3 priorities the night before or early in the morning. For each activity, ask yourself "Is there a smarter way to achieve the same outcome?

"The key to productivity is to rotate your avoidance techniques." --Shannon Wheeler

173

DAY: DAILY THEME:

Win the Day Planning

Today, I am grateful I get to be a coach because:

I have reviewed my team, recruiting, administrative & personal goals ☐

Today's Results List: List in priority order the top 3 things you can accomplish that would make a measurable impact on your goals and projects? What metric are you trying to hit? Schedule it.

Priority #1:   **Metric I am aiming for_____**

Priority #2:   **Metric I am aiming for_____**

Priority #3:   **Metric I am aiming for_____**

Person/People I need to Lead or Connect with Today (and How to Do It Well)

What or Who Am I Waiting On To Get a Project Done:

Who Needs Something From Me Today or This Week That I Can Proactively Get To Them?

○ **Morning Routine**   ○ **Workday Startup Routine**

TIME	DAILY SCHEDULE
5 am	
6 am	
7 am	
8 am	
9 am	
10 am	
11 am	
12 pm	
1 pm	
2 pm	
3 pm	
4 pm	
5 pm	
6 pm	
7 pm	
8 pm	
9 pm	
10 pm	
11 pm	

○ **Workday Shutdown Routine**   ○ **Evening Routine**

Staff meeting topics to cover:

Team meeting topics to cover:

THE DAILY TO-DO'S

Use this space to capture tasks, notes, or answer the questions: What happened in your day? What did you learn?

Recruiting:

Administrative

Calls/texts to make:

On Campus Visits:

Time Spent today

Social Media:

Events to Recruit at:

Time Spent today

Time Spent today

Team:

Personal:

Time Spent today

Time Spent today

PILE UP ZONE: Great ideas, goals, projects, apps or people to follow up on later

5 PERFORMANCE PILLARS	Give yourself a score of 1-5, 1=low and 5=high in terms of productivity					What could you do to get 1 point higher?
Mental Focus	1	2	3	4	5	
Mental/Emotional/Attitude	1	2	3	4	5	
Productivity	1	2	3	4	5	
Energy	1	2	3	4	5	
Social Connections	1	2	3	4	5	

Win tomorrow today: Plan your top 3 priorities the night before or early in the morning. For each activity, ask yourself "Is there a smarter way to achieve the same outcome?"

"It is not the strongest of the species that survive, nor the most intelligent, but the ones most responsive to change." --Charles Darwin

DAY: _____   DAILY THEME: _____

Win the Day Planning

Today, I am grateful I get to be a coach because:

_____

I have reviewed my team, recruiting, administrative & personal goals ☐

Today's Results List: List in priority order the top 3 things you can accomplish that would make a measurable impact on your goals and projects? What metric are you trying to hit? Schedule it.

Priority #1:   Metric I am aiming for_____

Priority #2:   Metric I am aiming for_____

Priority #3:   Metric I am aiming for_____

○ **Morning Routine**   ○ **Workday Startup Routine**

TIME	DAILY SCHEDULE
5 am	
6 am	
7 am	
8 am	
9 am	
10 am	
11 am	
12 pm	
1 pm	
2 pm	
3 pm	
4 pm	
5 pm	
6 pm	
7 pm	
8 pm	
9 pm	
10 pm	
11 pm	

○ **Workday Shutdown Routine**   ○ **Evening Routine**

Person/People I need to Lead or Connect with Today (and How to Do It Well)

Staff meeting topics to cover:

What or Who Am I Waiting On To Get a Project Done:

Team meeting topics to cover:

Who Needs Something From Me Today or This Week That I Can Proactively Get To Them?

THE DAILY TO-DO'S

Recruiting:	Administrative
Calls/texts to make:	
	Time Spent today
On Campus Visits:	Social Media:
Events to Recruit at:	
Time Spent today	Time Spent today
Team:	Personal:
Time Spent today	Time Spent today

PILE UP ZONE: Great ideas, goals, projects, apps or people to follow up on later

5 PERFORMANCE PILLARS	Give yourself a score of 1-5, 1=low and 5=high in terms of productivity					What could you do to get 1 point higher?
Mental Focus	1	2	3	4	5	
Mental/Emotional/Attitude	1	2	3	4	5	
Productivity	1	2	3	4	5	
Energy	1	2	3	4	5	
Social Connections	1	2	3	4	5	

Win tomorrow today: Plan your top 3 priorities the night before or early in the morning. For each activity, ask yourself "Is there a smarter way to achieve the same outcome?"

"Multitasking is a lie" --Gary Keller

DAY: DAILY THEME:

Win the Day Planning

Today, I am grateful I get to be a coach because:

I have reviewed my team, recruiting, administrative & personal goals ☐

Today's Results List: List in priority order the top 3 things you can accomplish that would make a measurable impact on your goals and projects? What metric are you trying to hit? Schedule it.

Priority #1:   **Metric I am aiming for_____**

Priority #2:   **Metric I am aiming for_____**

Priority #3:   **Metric I am aiming for_____**

○ **Morning Routine**   ○ **Workday Startup Routine**

TIME	DAILY SCHEDULE
5 am	
6 am	
7 am	
8 am	
9 am	
10 am	
11 am	
12 pm	
1 pm	
2 pm	
3 pm	
4 pm	
5 pm	
6 pm	
7 pm	
8 pm	
9 pm	
10 pm	
11 pm	

○ **Workday Shutdown Routine**   ○ **Evening Routine**

Person/People I need to Lead or Connect with Today (and How to Do It Well)

Staff meeting topics to cover:

What or Who Am I Waiting On To Get a Project Done:

Team meeting topics to cover:

Who Needs Something From Me Today or This Week That I Can Proactively Get To Them?

THE DAILY TO-DO'S

Recruiting:

Administrative

Calls/texts to make:

Time Spent today

On Campus Visits:

Social Media:

Events to Recruit at:

Time Spent today

Time Spent today

Team:

Personal:

Time Spent today

Time Spent today

PILE UP ZONE: Great ideas, goals, projects, apps or people to follow up on later

5 PERFORMANCE PILLARS	Give yourself a score of 1-5, 1=low and 5=high in terms of productivity					What could you do to get 1 point higher?
Mental Focus	1	2	3	4	5	
Mental/Emotional/Attitude	1	2	3	4	5	
Productivity	1	2	3	4	5	
Energy	1	2	3	4	5	
Social Connections	1	2	3	4	5	

Win tomorrow today: Plan your top 3 priorities the night before or early in the morning. For each activity, ask yourself "Is there a smarter way to achieve the same outcome?

"Do the hard jobs first. The easy jobs will take care of themselves." Dale Carnegie

DAY: DAILY THEME:

Win the Day Planning

Today, I am grateful I get to be a coach because:

I have reviewed my team, recruiting, administrative & personal goals ☐

Today's Results List: List in priority order the top 3 things you can accomplish that would make a measurable impact on your goals and projects? What metric are you trying to hit? Schedule it.

Priority #1:   **Metric I am aiming for_____**

Priority #2:   **Metric I am aiming for_____**

Priority #3:   **Metric I am aiming for_____**

Person/People I need to Lead or Connect with Today (and How to Do It Well)

What or Who Am I Waiting On To Get a Project Done:

Who Needs Something From Me Today or This Week That I Can Proactively Get To Them?

○ **Morning Routine**　　　　○ **Workday Startup Routine**

TIME	DAILY SCHEDULE
5 am	
6 am	
7 am	
8 am	
9 am	
10 am	
11 am	
12 pm	
1 pm	
2 pm	
3 pm	
4 pm	
5 pm	
6 pm	
7 pm	
8 pm	
9 pm	
10 pm	
11 pm	

○ **Workday Shutdown Routine**　　　　○ **Evening Routine**

Staff meeting topics to cover:

Team meeting topics to cover:

THE DAILY TO-DO'S

Recruiting:

Calls/texts to make:

On Campus Visits:

Events to Recruit at:

Time Spent today

Team:

Time Spent today

Administrative

Time Spent today

Social Media:

Time Spent today

Personal:

Time Spent today

PILE UP ZONE: Great ideas, goals, projects, apps or people to follow up on later

5 PERFORMANCE PILLARS	Give yourself a score of 1-5. 1=low and 5=high in terms of productivity					What could you do to get 1 point higher?
Mental Focus	1	2	3	4	5	
Mental/Emotional/Attitude	1	2	3	4	5	
Productivity	1	2	3	4	5	
Energy	1	2	3	4	5	
Social Connections	1	2	3	4	5	

Win tomorrow today: Plan your top 3 priorities the night before or early in the morning.   For each activity, ask yourself "Is there a smarter way to achieve the same outcome?"

"You can fool everyone else, but you can't fool your own mind." David Allen

DAY: DAILY THEME:

Win the Day Planning

Today, I am grateful I get to be a coach because:

I have reviewed my team, recruiting, administrative & personal goals   ☐

Today's Results List: List in priority order the top 3 things you can accomplish that would make a measurable impact on your goals and projects? What metric are you trying to hit? Schedule it.

Priority #1:   **Metric I am aiming for_____**

Priority #2:   **Metric I am aiming for_____**

Priority #3:   **Metric I am aiming for_____**

Person/People I need to Lead or Connect with Today (and How to Do It Well)

What or Who Am I Waiting On To Get a Project Done:

Who Needs Something From Me Today or This Week That I Can Proactively Get To Them?

○   **Morning Routine**   ○   **Workday Startup Routine**

TIME	DAILY SCHEDULE
5 am	
6 am	
7 am	
8 am	
9 am	
10 am	
11 am	
12 pm	
1 pm	
2 pm	
3 pm	
4 pm	
5 pm	
6 pm	
7 pm	
8 pm	
9 pm	
10 pm	
11 pm	

○   **Workday Shutdown Routine**   ○   **Evening Routine**

Staff meeting topics to cover:

Team meeting topics to cover:

THE DAILY TO-DO'S

Recruiting:

Administrative

Calls/texts to make:

Time Spent today

On Campus Visits:

Social Media:

Events to Recruit at:

Time Spent today

Time Spent today

Team:

Personal:

Time Spent today

Time Spent today

PILE UP ZONE: Great ideas, goals, projects, apps or people to follow up on later

5 PERFORMANCE PILLARS	Give yourself a score of 1-5, 1=low and 5=high in terms of productivity					What could you do to get 1 point higher?
Mental Focus	1	2	3	4	5	
Mental/Emotional/Attitude	1	2	3	4	5	
Productivity	1	2	3	4	5	
Energy	1	2	3	4	5	
Social Connections	1	2	3	4	5	

Win tomorrow today: Plan your top 3 priorities the night before or early in the morning.   For each activity, ask yourself "Is there a smarter way to achieve the same outcome?

"You miss 100% of the shots you don't take." Wayne Gretzky

183

DAY: DAILY THEME:

Win the Day Planning

Today, I am grateful I get to be a coach because:

I have reviewed my team, recruiting, administrative & personal goals ☐

Today's Results List: List in priority order the top 3 things you can accomplish that would make a measurable impact on your goals and projects? What metric are you trying to hit? Schedule it.

Priority #1:   Metric I am aiming for_____

Priority #2:   Metric I am aiming for_____

Priority #3:   Metric I am aiming for_____

○ **Morning Routine**   ○ **Workday Startup Routine**

TIME	DAILY SCHEDULE
5 am	
6 am	
7 am	
8 am	
9 am	
10 am	
11 am	
12 pm	
1 pm	
2 pm	
3 pm	
4 pm	
5 pm	
6 pm	
7 pm	
8 pm	
9 pm	
10 pm	
11 pm	

○ **Workday Shutdown Routine**   ○ **Evening Routine**

Person/People I need to Lead or Connect with Today (and How to Do It Well)

Staff meeting topics to cover:

What or Who Am I Waiting On To Get a Project Done:

Team meeting topics to cover:

Who Needs Something From Me Today or This Week That I Can Proactively Get To Them?

THE DAILY TO-DO'S

Recruiting:

Calls/texts to make:

On Campus Visits:

Events to Recruit at:

Time Spent today

Administrative

Time Spent today

Social Media:

Time Spent today

Team:

Time Spent today

Personal:

Time Spent today

PILE UP ZONE: Great ideas, goals, projects, apps or people to follow up on later

5 PERFORMANCE PILLARS	Give yourself a score of 1-5, 1=low and 5=high in terms of productivity					What could you do to get 1 point higher?
Mental Focus	1	2	3	4	5	
Mental/Emotional/Attitude	1	2	3	4	5	
Productivity	1	2	3	4	5	
Energy	1	2	3	4	5	
Social Connections	1	2	3	4	5	

Win tomorrow today: Plan your top 3 priorities the night before or early in the morning.   For each activity, ask yourself "Is there a smarter way to achieve the same outcome?

"The only thing to do with good advice is to pass it on. It is never of any use to oneself." Oscar Wilde

DAY: DAILY THEME:

Win the Day Planning

Today, I am grateful I get to be a coach because:

I have reviewed my team, recruiting, administrative & personal goals ☐

Today's Results List: List in priority order the top 3 things you can accomplish that would make a measurable impact on your goals and projects? What metric are you trying to hit? Schedule it.

Priority #1:   **Metric I am aiming for_____**

Priority #2:   **Metric I am aiming for_____**

Priority #3:   **Metric I am aiming for_____**

○ **Morning Routine**   ○ **Workday Startup Routine**

TIME	DAILY SCHEDULE
5 am	
6 am	
7 am	
8 am	
9 am	
10 am	
11 am	
12 pm	
1 pm	
2 pm	
3 pm	
4 pm	
5 pm	
6 pm	
7 pm	
8 pm	
9 pm	
10 pm	
11 pm	

○ **Workday Shutdown Routine**   ○ **Evening Routine**

Person/People I need to Lead or Connect with Today (and How to Do It Well)

Staff meeting topics to cover:

What or Who Am I Waiting On To Get a Project Done:

Team meeting topics to cover:

Who Needs Something From Me Today or This Week That I Can Proactively Get To Them?

THE DAILY TO-DO'S

Recruiting:

Calls/texts to make:

On Campus Visits:

Events to Recruit at:

Time Spent today

Administrative

Time Spent today

Social Media:

Time Spent today

Team:

Time Spent today

Personal:

Time Spent today

PILE UP ZONE: Great ideas, goals, projects, apps or people to follow up on later

5 PERFORMANCE PILLARS	Give yourself a score of 1-5, 1=low and 5=high in terms of productivity					What could you do to get 1 point higher?
Mental Focus	1	2	3	4	5	
Mental/Emotional/Attitude	1	2	3	4	5	
Productivity	1	2	3	4	5	
Energy	1	2	3	4	5	
Social Connections	1	2	3	4	5	

Win tomorrow today: Plan your top 3 priorities the night before or early in the morning. For each activity, ask yourself "Is there a smarter way to achieve the same outcome?"

"Why do anything unless it is going to be great?" Peter Block

DAY: DAILY THEME:

Win the Day Planning

Today, I am grateful I get to be a coach because:

I have reviewed my team, recruiting, administrative & personal goals ☐

Today's Results List: List in priority order the top 3 things you can accomplish that would make a measurable impact on your goals and projects? What metric are you trying to hit? Schedule it.

Priority #1:   **Metric I am aiming for_____**

Priority #2:   **Metric I am aiming for_____**

Priority #3:   **Metric I am aiming for_____**

Person/People I need to Lead or Connect with Today (and How to Do It Well)

What or Who Am I Waiting On To Get a Project Done:

Who Needs Something From Me Today or This Week That I Can Proactively Get To Them?

○ **Morning Routine**   ○ **Workday Startup Routine**

TIME	DAILY SCHEDULE
5 am	
6 am	
7 am	
8 am	
9 am	
10 am	
11 am	
12 pm	
1 pm	
2 pm	
3 pm	
4 pm	
5 pm	
6 pm	
7 pm	
8 pm	
9 pm	
10 pm	
11 pm	

○ **Workday Shutdown Routine**   ○ **Evening Routine**

Staff meeting topics to cover:

Team meeting topics to cover:

THE DAILY TO-DO'S

Recruiting:

Administrative

Calls/texts to make:

Time Spent today

On Campus Visits:

Social Media:

Events to Recruit at:

Time Spent today

Time Spent today

Team:

Personal:

Time Spent today

Time Spent today

PILE UP ZONE: Great ideas, goals, projects, apps or people to follow up on later

5 PERFORMANCE PILLARS	Give yourself a score of 1-5, 1=low and 5=high in terms of productivity					What could you do to get 1 point higher?
Mental Focus	1	2	3	4	5	
Mental/Emotional/Attitude	1	2	3	4	5	
Productivity	1	2	3	4	5	
Energy	1	2	3	4	5	
Social Connections	1	2	3	4	5	

Win tomorrow today: Plan your top 3 priorities the night before or early in the morning. For each activity, ask yourself "Is there a smarter way to achieve the same outcome?

"Work gives you meaning and purpose and life is empty without it." Stephen Hawking

DAY: _____   DAILY THEME: _____

Win the Day Planning

Today, I am grateful I get to be a coach because:

I have reviewed my team, recruiting, administrative & personal goals ☐

Today's Results List: List in priority order the top 3 things you can accomplish that would make a measurable impact on your goals and projects? What metric are you trying to hit? Schedule it.

Priority #1:   **Metric I am aiming for_____**

Priority #2:   **Metric I am aiming for_____**

Priority #3:   **Metric I am aiming for_____**

Person/People I need to Lead or Connect with Today (and How to Do It Well)

What or Who Am I Waiting On To Get a Project Done:

Who Needs Something From Me Today or This Week That I Can Proactively Get To Them?

○ **Morning Routine**   ○ **Workday Startup Routine**

TIME	DAILY SCHEDULE
5 am	
6 am	
7 am	
8 am	
9 am	
10 am	
11 am	
12 pm	
1 pm	
2 pm	
3 pm	
4 pm	
5 pm	
6 pm	
7 pm	
8 pm	
9 pm	
10 pm	
11 pm	

○ **Workday Shutdown Routine**   ○ **Evening Routine**

Staff meeting topics to cover:

Team meeting topics to cover:

THE DAILY TO-DO'S

Recruiting:

Calls/texts to make:

On Campus Visits:

Events to Recruit at:

| Time Spent today |

Team:

| Time Spent today |

Administrative

| Time Spent today |

Social Media:

| Time Spent today |

Personal:

| Time Spent today |

PILE UP ZONE: Great ideas, goals, projects, apps or people to follow up on later

5 PERFORMANCE PILLARS	Give yourself a score of 1-5, 1=low and 5=high in terms of productivity					What could you do to get 1 point higher?
Mental Focus	1	2	3	4	5	
Mental/Emotional/Attitude	1	2	3	4	5	
Productivity	1	2	3	4	5	
Energy	1	2	3	4	5	
Social Connections	1	2	3	4	5	

Win tomorrow today: Plan your top 3 priorities the night before or early in the morning. For each activity, ask yourself "Is there a smarter way to achieve the same outcome?

Procrastinating is a vice when it comes to productivity, but it can be a virtue for creativity.– Adam Grant

DAY: _____   DAILY THEME: _____

Win the Day Planning

Today, I am grateful I get to be a coach because:

I have reviewed my team, recruiting, administrative & personal goals ☐

Today's Results List: List in priority order the top 3 things you can accomplish that would make a measurable impact on your goals and projects? What metric are you trying to hit? Schedule it.

Priority #1:   Metric I am aiming for_____

Priority #2:   Metric I am aiming for_____

Priority #3:   Metric I am aiming for_____

○ **Morning Routine**   ○ **Workday Startup Routine**

TIME	DAILY SCHEDULE
5 am	
6 am	
7 am	
8 am	
9 am	
10 am	
11 am	
12 pm	
1 pm	
2 pm	
3 pm	
4 pm	
5 pm	
6 pm	
7 pm	
8 pm	
9 pm	
10 pm	
11 pm	

○ **Workday Shutdown Routine**   ○ **Evening Routine**

Person/People I need to Lead or Connect with Today (and How to Do It Well)

Staff meeting topics to cover:

What or Who Am I Waiting On To Get a Project Done:

Team meeting topics to cover:

Who Needs Something From Me Today or This Week That I Can Proactively Get To Them?

THE DAILY TO-DO'S

Recruiting:

Administrative

Calls/texts to make:

Time Spent today

On Campus Visits:

Social Media:

Events to Recruit at:

Time Spent today

Time Spent today

Team:

Personal:

Time Spent today

Time Spent today

PILE UP ZONE: Great ideas, goals, projects, apps or people to follow up on later

5 PERFORMANCE PILLARS	Give yourself a score of 1-5, 1=low and 5=high in terms of productivity					What could you do to get 1 point higher?
Mental Focus	1	2	3	4	5	
Mental/Emotional/Attitude	1	2	3	4	5	
Productivity	1	2	3	4	5	
Energy	1	2	3	4	5	
Social Connections	1	2	3	4	5	

Win tomorrow today: Plan your top 3 priorities the night before or early in the morning. For each activity, ask yourself "Is there a smarter way to achieve the same outcome?

Happiness, the feeling of positivity, really is the foundation of productivity.– Miguel McKelvey

DAY: _____   DAILY THEME: _____

Win the Day Planning

Today, I am grateful I get to be a coach because:

I have reviewed my team, recruiting, administrative & personal goals ☐

Today's Results List: List in priority order the top 3 things you can accomplish that would make a measurable impact on your goals and projects? What metric are you trying to hit? Schedule it.

Priority #1:   Metric I am aiming for_____

Priority #2:   Metric I am aiming for_____

Priority #3:   Metric I am aiming for_____

Person/People I need to Lead or Connect with Today (and How to Do It Well)

What or Who Am I Waiting On To Get a Project Done:

Who Needs Something From Me Today or This Week That I Can Proactively Get To Them?

○ **Morning Routine**   ○ **Workday Startup Routine**

TIME	DAILY SCHEDULE
5 am	
6 am	
7 am	
8 am	
9 am	
10 am	
11 am	
12 pm	
1 pm	
2 pm	
3 pm	
4 pm	
5 pm	
6 pm	
7 pm	
8 pm	
9 pm	
10 pm	
11 pm	

○ **Workday Shutdown Routine**   ○ **Evening Routine**

Staff meeting topics to cover:

Team meeting topics to cover:

THE DAILY TO-DO'S

Recruiting:

Calls/texts to make:

On Campus Visits:

Events to Recruit at:

Time Spent today

Team:

Time Spent today

Administrative

Time Spent today

Social Media:

Time Spent today

Personal:

Time Spent today

PILE UP ZONE: Great ideas, goals, projects, apps or people to follow up on later

5 PERFORMANCE PILLARS	Give yourself a score of 1-5, 1=low and 5=high in terms of productivity					What could you do to get 1 point higher?
Mental Focus	1	2	3	4	5	
Mental/Emotional/Attitude	1	2	3	4	5	
Productivity	1	2	3	4	5	
Energy	1	2	3	4	5	
Social Connections	1	2	3	4	5	

Win tomorrow today: Plan your top 3 priorities the night before or early in the morning.   For each activity, ask yourself "Is there a smarter way to achieve the same outcome?

When you care about people's happiness and productivity, you give them what brings out the best in them and their creativity.— Tim Cook

DAY: DAILY THEME:

Win the Day Planning

Today, I am grateful I get to be a coach because:

I have reviewed my team, recruiting, administrative & personal goals ☐

Today's Results List: List in priority order the top 3 things you can accomplish that would make a measurable impact on your goals and projects? What metric are you trying to hit? Schedule it.

Priority #1:   **Metric I am aiming for_____**

Priority #2:   **Metric I am aiming for_____**

Priority #3:   **Metric I am aiming for_____**

Person/People I need to Lead or Connect with Today (and How to Do It Well)

What or Who Am I Waiting On To Get a Project Done:

Who Needs Something From Me Today or This Week That I Can Proactively Get To Them?

○ **Morning Routine**   ○ **Workday Startup Routine**

TIME	DAILY SCHEDULE
5 am	
6 am	
7 am	
8 am	
9 am	
10 am	
11 am	
12 pm	
1 pm	
2 pm	
3 pm	
4 pm	
5 pm	
6 pm	
7 pm	
8 pm	
9 pm	
10 pm	
11 pm	

○ **Workday Shutdown Routine**   ○ **Evening Routine**

Staff meeting topics to cover:

Team meeting topics to cover:

THE DAILY TO-DO'S

Recruiting:

Administrative

Calls/texts to make:

Time Spent today

On Campus Visits:

Social Media:

Events to Recruit at:

Time Spent today

Time Spent today

Team:

Personal:

Time Spent today

Time Spent today

PILE UP ZONE: Great ideas, goals, projects, apps or people to follow up on later

5 PERFORMANCE PILLARS	Give yourself a score of 1-5, 1=low and 5=high in terms of productivity					What could you do to get 1 point higher?
Mental Focus	1	2	3	4	5	
Mental/Emotional/Attitude	1	2	3	4	5	
Productivity	1	2	3	4	5	
Energy	1	2	3	4	5	
Social Connections	1	2	3	4	5	

Win tomorrow today: Plan your top 3 priorities the night before or early in the morning. For each activity, ask yourself "Is there a smarter way to achieve the same outcome?

The more you eliminate the inefficient use of information, the better it is for productivity.– Mitch Kapor

DAY: _____   DAILY THEME: _____

Win the Day Planning

Today, I am grateful I get to be a coach because:

I have reviewed my team, recruiting, administrative & personal goals ☐

Today's Results List: List in priority order the top 3 things you can accomplish that would make a measurable impact on your goals and projects? What metric are you trying to hit? Schedule it.

Priority #1:   Metric I am aiming for_____

Priority #2:   Metric I am aiming for_____

Priority #3:   Metric I am aiming for_____

Person/People I need to Lead or Connect with Today (and How to Do It Well)

What or Who Am I Waiting On To Get a Project Done:

Who Needs Something From Me Today or This Week That I Can Proactively Get To Them?

○ **Morning Routine**   ○ **Workday Startup Routine**

TIME	DAILY SCHEDULE
5 am	
6 am	
7 am	
8 am	
9 am	
10 am	
11 am	
12 pm	
1 pm	
2 pm	
3 pm	
4 pm	
5 pm	
6 pm	
7 pm	
8 pm	
9 pm	
10 pm	
11 pm	

○ **Workday Shutdown Routine**   ○ **Evening Routine**

Staff meeting topics to cover:

Team meeting topics to cover:

THE DAILY TO-DO'S

Recruiting:

Administrative

Calls/texts to make:

Time Spent today

On Campus Visits:

Social Media:

Events to Recruit at:

Time Spent today

Time Spent today

Team:

Personal:

Time Spent today

Time Spent today

PILE UP ZONE: Great ideas, goals, projects, apps or people to follow up on later

5 PERFORMANCE PILLARS	Give yourself a score of 1-5, 1=low and 5=high in terms of productivity					What could you do to get 1 point higher?
Mental Focus	1	2	3	4	5	
Mental/Emotional/Attitude	1	2	3	4	5	
Productivity	1	2	3	4	5	
Energy	1	2	3	4	5	
Social Connections	1	2	3	4	5	

Win tomorrow today: Plan your top 3 priorities the night before or early in the morning. For each activity, ask yourself "Is there a smarter way to achieve the same outcome?

"There is little that the human mind can conceive that is not possible of accomplishment." – Charles Schwab

DAY: _____   DAILY THEME: _____

Win the Day Planning

Today, I am grateful I get to be a coach because:

I have reviewed my team, recruiting, administrative & personal goals ☐

Today's Results List: List in priority order the top 3 things you can accomplish that would make a measurable impact on your goals and projects? What metric are you trying to hit? Schedule it.

Priority #1:   **Metric I am aiming for_____**

Priority #2:   **Metric I am aiming for_____**

Priority #3:   **Metric I am aiming for_____**

Person/People I need to Lead or Connect with Today (and How to Do It Well)

What or Who Am I Waiting On To Get a Project Done:

Who Needs Something From Me Today or This Week That I Can Proactively Get To Them?

○ **Morning Routine**   ○ **Workday Startup Routine**

TIME	DAILY SCHEDULE
5 am	
6 am	
7 am	
8 am	
9 am	
10 am	
11 am	
12 pm	
1 pm	
2 pm	
3 pm	
4 pm	
5 pm	
6 pm	
7 pm	
8 pm	
9 pm	
10 pm	
11 pm	

○ **Workday Shutdown Routine**   ○ **Evening Routine**

Staff meeting topics to cover:

Team meeting topics to cover:

THE DAILY TO-DO'S

Recruiting:

Calls/texts to make:

On Campus Visits:

Events to Recruit at:

Time Spent today

Administrative

Time Spent today

Social Media:

Time Spent today

Team:

Time Spent today

Personal:

Time Spent today

PILE UP ZONE: Great ideas, goals, projects, apps or people to follow up on later

5 PERFORMANCE PILLARS	Give yourself a score of 1-5. 1=low and 5=high in terms of productivity					What could you do to get 1 point higher?
Mental Focus	1	2	3	4	5	
Mental/Emotional/Attitude	1	2	3	4	5	
Productivity	1	2	3	4	5	
Energy	1	2	3	4	5	
Social Connections	1	2	3	4	5	

Win tomorrow today: Plan your top 3 priorities the night before or early in the morning. For each activity, ask yourself "Is there a smarter way to achieve the same outcome?

"Drive thy business or it will drive thee." – Benjamin Franklin

DAY: DAILY THEME:

Win the Day Planning

Today, I am grateful I get to be a coach because:

I have reviewed my team, recruiting, administrative & personal goals ☐

Today's Results List: List in priority order the top 3 things you can accomplish that would make a measurable impact on your goals and projects? What metric are you trying to hit? Schedule it.

Priority #1:   **Metric I am aiming for_____**

Priority #2:   **Metric I am aiming for_____**

Priority #3:   **Metric I am aiming for_____**

○ **Morning Routine**   ○ **Workday Startup Routine**

TIME	DAILY SCHEDULE
5 am	
6 am	
7 am	
8 am	
9 am	
10 am	
11 am	
12 pm	
1 pm	
2 pm	
3 pm	
4 pm	
5 pm	
6 pm	
7 pm	
8 pm	
9 pm	
10 pm	
11 pm	

○ **Workday Shutdown Routine**   ○ **Evening Routine**

Staff meeting topics to cover:

Person/People I need to Lead or Connect with Today (and How to Do It Well)

What or Who Am I Waiting On To Get a Project Done:

Team meeting topics to cover:

Who Needs Something From Me Today or This Week That I Can Proactively Get To Them?

THE DAILY TO-DO'S

Recruiting:

Administrative

Calls/texts to make:

Time Spent today

On Campus Visits:

Social Media:

Events to Recruit at:

Time Spent today

Time Spent today

Team:

Personal:

Time Spent today

Time Spent today

PILE UP ZONE: Great ideas, goals, projects, apps or people to follow up on later

5 PERFORMANCE PILLARS	Give yourself a score of 1-5, 1=low and 5=high in terms of productivity					What could you do to get 1 point higher?
Mental Focus	1	2	3	4	5	
Mental/Emotional/Attitude	1	2	3	4	5	
Productivity	1	2	3	4	5	
Energy	1	2	3	4	5	
Social Connections	1	2	3	4	5	

Win tomorrow today: Plan your top 3 priorities the night before or early in the morning. For each activity, ask yourself "Is there a smarter way to achieve the same outcome?"

"Effective performance is preceded by painstaking preparation" – Brian Tracy

DAY: DAILY THEME:

	Win the Day Planning

Today, I am grateful I get to be a coach because:

I have reviewed my team, recruiting, administrative & personal goals ☐

Today's Results List: List in priority order the top 3 things you can accomplish that would make a measurable impact on your goals and projects? What metric are you trying to hit? Schedule it.

Priority #1:   **Metric I am aiming for_____**

Priority #2:   **Metric I am aiming for_____**

Priority #3:   **Metric I am aiming for_____**

Person/People I need to Lead or Connect with Today (and How to Do It Well)

What or Who Am I Waiting On To Get a Project Done:

Who Needs Something From Me Today or This Week That I Can Proactively Get To Them?

○ **Morning Routine**   ○ **Workday Startup Routine**

TIME	DAILY SCHEDULE
5 am	
6 am	
7 am	
8 am	
9 am	
10 am	
11 am	
12 pm	
1 pm	
2 pm	
3 pm	
4 pm	
5 pm	
6 pm	
7 pm	
8 pm	
9 pm	
10 pm	
11 pm	

○ **Workday Shutdown Routine**   ○ **Evening Routine**

Staff meeting topics to cover:

Team meeting topics to cover:

THE DAILY TO-DO'S

Recruiting:

Calls/texts to make:

On Campus Visits:

Events to Recruit at:

Time Spent today

Team:

Time Spent today

Administrative

Time Spent today

Social Media:

Time Spent today

Personal:

Time Spent today

PILE UP ZONE: Great ideas, goals, projects, apps or people to follow up on later

5 PERFORMANCE PILLARS	Give yourself a score of 1-5, 1=low and 5=high in terms of productivity					What could you do to get 1 point higher?
Mental Focus	1	2	3	4	5	
Mental/Emotional/Attitude	1	2	3	4	5	
Productivity	1	2	3	4	5	
Energy	1	2	3	4	5	
Social Connections	1	2	3	4	5	

Win tomorrow today: Plan your top 3 priorities the night before or early in the morning. For each activity, ask yourself "Is there a smarter way to achieve the same outcome?

"What we fear doing most is usually what we most need to do." – Tim Ferriss

DAY: DAILY THEME:

Win the Day Planning	○ **Morning Routine** ○ **Workday Startup Routine**

Today, I am grateful I get to be a coach because:

I have reviewed my team, recruiting, administrative & personal goals ☐

Today's Results List: List in priority order the top 3 things you can accomplish that would make a measurable impact on your goals and projects? What metric are you trying to hit? Schedule it.

Priority #1:   **Metric I am aiming for_____**

Priority #2:   **Metric I am aiming for_____**

Priority #3:   **Metric I am aiming for_____**

TIME	DAILY SCHEDULE
5 am	
6 am	
7 am	
8 am	
9 am	
10 am	
11 am	
12 pm	
1 pm	
2 pm	
3 pm	
4 pm	
5 pm	
6 pm	
7 pm	
8 pm	
9 pm	
10 pm	
11 pm	

○ **Workday Shutdown Routine**   ○ **Evening Routine**

Person/People I need to Lead or Connect with Today (and How to Do It Well)

Staff meeting topics to cover:

What or Who Am I Waiting On To Get a Project Done:

Team meeting topics to cover:

Who Needs Something From Me Today or This Week That I Can Proactively Get To Them?

THE DAILY TO-DO'S

Recruiting:

Calls/texts to make:

On Campus Visits:

Events to Recruit at:

Time Spent today

Team:

Time Spent today

Administrative

Time Spent today

Social Media:

Time Spent today

Personal:

Time Spent today

PILE UP ZONE: Great ideas, goals, projects, apps or people to follow up on later

5 PERFORMANCE PILLARS	Give yourself a score of 1-5, 1=low and 5=high in terms of productivity					What could you do to get 1 point higher?
Mental Focus	1	2	3	4	5	
Mental/Emotional/Attitude	1	2	3	4	5	
Productivity	1	2	3	4	5	
Energy	1	2	3	4	5	
Social Connections	1	2	3	4	5	

Win tomorrow today: Plan your top 3 priorities the night before or early in the morning. For each activity, ask yourself "Is there a smarter way to achieve the same outcome?"

"To be disciplined is to follow in a good way. To be self-disciplined is to follow in a better way." – Corita Kent

207

DAY: DAILY THEME:

Win the Day Planning

Today, I am grateful I get to be a coach because:

I have reviewed my team, recruiting, administrative & personal goals ☐

Today's Results List: List in priority order the top 3 things you can accomplish that would make a measurable impact on your goals and projects? What metric are you trying to hit? Schedule it.

Priority #1:   **Metric I am aiming for_____**

Priority #2:   **Metric I am aiming for_____**

Priority #3:   **Metric I am aiming for_____**

Person/People I need to Lead or Connect with Today (and How to Do It Well)

What or Who Am I Waiting On To Get a Project Done:

Who Needs Something From Me Today or This Week That I Can Proactively Get To Them?

○ **Morning Routine**   ○ **Workday Startup Routine**

TIME	DAILY SCHEDULE
5 am	
6 am	
7 am	
8 am	
9 am	
10 am	
11 am	
12 pm	
1 pm	
2 pm	
3 pm	
4 pm	
5 pm	
6 pm	
7 pm	
8 pm	
9 pm	
10 pm	
11 pm	

○ **Workday Shutdown Routine**   ○ **Evening Routine**

Staff meeting topics to cover:

Team meeting topics to cover:

THE DAILY TO-DO'S

Recruiting:	Administrative
Calls/texts to make:	
	Time Spent today
On Campus Visits:	Social Media:
Events to Recruit at:	
Time Spent today	Time Spent today
Team:	Personal:
Time Spent today	Time Spent today

PILE UP ZONE: Great ideas, goals, projects, apps or people to follow up on later

5 PERFORMANCE PILLARS	Give yourself a score of 1-5. 1=low and 5=high in terms of productivity					What could you do to get 1 point higher?
Mental Focus	1	2	3	4	5	
Mental/Emotional/Attitude	1	2	3	4	5	
Productivity	1	2	3	4	5	
Energy	1	2	3	4	5	
Social Connections	1	2	3	4	5	

Win tomorrow today: Plan your top 3 priorities the night before or early in the morning. For each activity, ask yourself "Is there a smarter way to achieve the same outcome?

"The least productive people are usually the ones who are most in favor of holding meetings." – Thomas Sowell

DAY: _____   DAILY THEME: _____

Win the Day Planning

Today, I am grateful I get to be a coach because:

I have reviewed my team, recruiting, administrative & personal goals ☐

Today's Results List: List in priority order the top 3 things you can accomplish that would make a measurable impact on your goals and projects? What metric are you trying to hit? Schedule it.

Priority #1:   Metric I am aiming for_____

Priority #2:   Metric I am aiming for_____

Priority #3:   Metric I am aiming for_____

Person/People I need to Lead or Connect with Today (and How to Do It Well)

What or Who Am I Waiting On To Get a Project Done:

Who Needs Something From Me Today or This Week That I Can Proactively Get To Them?

○ **Morning Routine**   ○ **Workday Startup Routine**

TIME	DAILY SCHEDULE
5 am	
6 am	
7 am	
8 am	
9 am	
10 am	
11 am	
12 pm	
1 pm	
2 pm	
3 pm	
4 pm	
5 pm	
6 pm	
7 pm	
8 pm	
9 pm	
10 pm	
11 pm	

○ **Workday Shutdown Routine**   ○ **Evening Routine**

Staff meeting topics to cover:

Team meeting topics to cover:

THE DAILY TO-DO'S

Recruiting:

Administrative

Calls/texts to make:

Time Spent today

On Campus Visits:

Social Media:

Events to Recruit at:

Time Spent today

Time Spent today

Team:

Personal:

Time Spent today

Time Spent today

PILE UP ZONE: Great ideas, goals, projects, apps or people to follow up on later

5 PERFORMANCE PILLARS	Give yourself a score of 1-5, 1=low and 5=high in terms of productivity					What could you do to get 1 point higher?
Mental Focus	1	2	3	4	5	
Mental/Emotional/Attitude	1	2	3	4	5	
Productivity	1	2	3	4	5	
Energy	1	2	3	4	5	
Social Connections	1	2	3	4	5	

Win tomorrow today: Plan your top 3 priorities the night before or early in the morning. For each activity, ask yourself "Is there a smarter way to achieve the same outcome?

"To do two things at once is to do neither." – Publius Syrus

DAY: DAILY THEME:

	Win the Day Planning

Today, I am grateful I get to be a coach because:

I have reviewed my team, recruiting, administrative & personal goals ☐

Today's Results List: List in priority order the top 3 things you can accomplish that would make a measurable impact on your goals and projects? What metric are you trying to hit? Schedule it.

Priority #1:   **Metric I am aiming for_____**

Priority #2:   **Metric I am aiming for_____**

Priority #3:   **Metric I am aiming for_____**

Person/People I need to Lead or Connect with Today (and How to Do It Well)

What or Who Am I Waiting On To Get a Project Done:

Who Needs Something From Me Today or This Week That I Can Proactively Get To Them?

○ **Morning Routine**   ○ **Workday Startup Routine**

TIME	DAILY SCHEDULE
5 am	
6 am	
7 am	
8 am	
9 am	
10 am	
11 am	
12 pm	
1 pm	
2 pm	
3 pm	
4 pm	
5 pm	
6 pm	
7 pm	
8 pm	
9 pm	
10 pm	
11 pm	

○ **Workday Shutdown Routine**   ○ **Evening Routine**

Staff meeting topics to cover:

Team meeting topics to cover:

THE DAILY TO-DO'S

Recruiting:

Calls/texts to make:

On Campus Visits:

Events to Recruit at:

Time Spent today

Administrative

Time Spent today

Social Media:

Time Spent today

Team:

Time Spent today

Personal:

Time Spent today

PILE UP ZONE: Great ideas, goals, projects, apps or people to follow up on later

5 PERFORMANCE PILLARS	Give yourself a score of 1-5, 1=low and 5=high in terms of productivity					What could you do to get 1 point higher?
Mental Focus	1	2	3	4	5	
Mental/Emotional/Attitude	1	2	3	4	5	
Productivity	1	2	3	4	5	
Energy	1	2	3	4	5	
Social Connections	1	2	3	4	5	

Win tomorrow today: Plan your top 3 priorities the night before or early in the morning. For each activity, ask yourself "Is there a smarter way to achieve the same outcome?

"Anyone who has never made a mistake has never tried anything new." – Albert Einstein

DAY: DAILY THEME:

Win the Day Planning

Today, I am grateful I get to be a coach because:

I have reviewed my team, recruiting, administrative & personal goals ☐

Today's Results List: List in priority order the top 3 things you can accomplish that would make a measurable impact on your goals and projects? What metric are you trying to hit? Schedule it.

Priority #1:   Metric I am aiming for_____

Priority #2:   Metric I am aiming for_____

Priority #3:   Metric I am aiming for_____

○ **Morning Routine**   ○ **Workday Startup Routine**

TIME	DAILY SCHEDULE
5 am	
6 am	
7 am	
8 am	
9 am	
10 am	
11 am	
12 pm	
1 pm	
2 pm	
3 pm	
4 pm	
5 pm	
6 pm	
7 pm	
8 pm	
9 pm	
10 pm	
11 pm	

○ **Workday Shutdown Routine**   ○ **Evening Routine**

Person/People I need to Lead or Connect with Today (and How to Do It Well)

Staff meeting topics to cover:

What or Who Am I Waiting On To Get a Project Done:

Team meeting topics to cover:

Who Needs Something From Me Today or This Week That I Can Proactively Get To Them?

THE DAILY TO-DO'S

Recruiting:	Administrative
Calls/texts to make:	
	Time Spent today
On Campus Visits:	Social Media:
Events to Recruit at:	
Time Spent today	Time Spent today
Team:	Personal:
Time Spent today	Time Spent today

PILE UP ZONE: Great ideas, goals, projects, apps or people to follow up on later

5 PERFORMANCE PILLARS	Give yourself a score of 1-5, 1=low and 5=high in terms of productivity					What could you do to get 1 point higher?
Mental Focus	1	2	3	4	5	
Mental/Emotional/Attitude	1	2	3	4	5	
Productivity	1	2	3	4	5	
Energy	1	2	3	4	5	
Social Connections	1	2	3	4	5	

Win tomorrow today: Plan your top 3 priorities the night before or early in the morning.   For each activity, ask yourself "Is there a smarter way to achieve the same outcome?"

"Soon is not as good as now." – Seth Godin

DAY: DAILY THEME:

Win the Day Planning

Today, I am grateful I get to be a coach because:

I have reviewed my team, recruiting, administrative & personal goals ☐

Today's Results List: List in priority order the top 3 things you can accomplish that would make a measurable impact on your goals and projects? What metric are you trying to hit? Schedule it.

Priority #1:   **Metric I am aiming for_____**

Priority #2:   **Metric I am aiming for_____**

Priority #3:   **Metric I am aiming for_____**

Person/People I need to Lead or Connect with Today (and How to Do It Well)

What or Who Am I Waiting On To Get a Project Done:

Who Needs Something From Me Today or This Week That I Can Proactively Get To Them?

○ **Morning Routine**   ○ **Workday Startup Routine**

TIME	DAILY SCHEDULE
5 am	
6 am	
7 am	
8 am	
9 am	
10 am	
11 am	
12 pm	
1 pm	
2 pm	
3 pm	
4 pm	
5 pm	
6 pm	
7 pm	
8 pm	
9 pm	
10 pm	
11 pm	

○ **Workday Shutdown Routine**   ○ **Evening Routine**

Staff meeting topics to cover:

Team meeting topics to cover:

THE DAILY TO-DO'S

Recruiting:

Calls/texts to make:

On Campus Visits:

Events to Recruit at:

Time Spent today

Administrative

Time Spent today

Social Media:

Time Spent today

Team:

Time Spent today

Personal:

Time Spent today

PILE UP ZONE: Great ideas, goals, projects, apps or people to follow up on later

5 PERFORMANCE PILLARS	Give yourself a score of 1-5. 1=low and 5=high in terms of productivity					What could you do to get 1 point higher?
Mental Focus	1	2	3	4	5	
Mental/Emotional/Attitude	1	2	3	4	5	
Productivity	1	2	3	4	5	
Energy	1	2	3	4	5	
Social Connections	1	2	3	4	5	

Win tomorrow today: Plan your top 3 priorities the night before or early in the morning. For each activity, ask yourself "Is there a smarter way to achieve the same outcome?

"Always deliver more than expected." Larry Page

DAY: _____   DAILY THEME: _____

Win the Day Planning

Today, I am grateful I get to be a coach because:

I have reviewed my team, recruiting, administrative & personal goals ☐

Today's Results List: List in priority order the top 3 things you can accomplish that would make a measurable impact on your goals and projects? What metric are you trying to hit? Schedule it.

Priority #1:   Metric I am aiming for_____

Priority #2:   Metric I am aiming for_____

Priority #3:   Metric I am aiming for_____

○ **Morning Routine**   ○ **Workday Startup Routine**

TIME	DAILY SCHEDULE
5 am	
6 am	
7 am	
8 am	
9 am	
10 am	
11 am	
12 pm	
1 pm	
2 pm	
3 pm	
4 pm	
5 pm	
6 pm	
7 pm	
8 pm	
9 pm	
10 pm	
11 pm	

○ **Workday Shutdown Routine**   ○ **Evening Routine**

Person/People I need to Lead or Connect with Today (and How to Do It Well)

Staff meeting topics to cover:

What or Who Am I Waiting On To Get a Project Done:

Team meeting topics to cover:

Who Needs Something From Me Today or This Week That I Can Proactively Get To Them?

THE DAILY TO-DO'S

Recruiting:

Calls/texts to make:

On Campus Visits:

Events to Recruit at:

Time Spent today

Team:

Time Spent today

Administrative

Time Spent today

Social Media:

Time Spent today

Personal:

Time Spent today

PILE UP ZONE: Great ideas, goals, projects, apps or people to follow up on later

5 PERFORMANCE PILLARS	Give yourself a score of 1-5, 1=low and 5=high in terms of productivity					What could you do to get 1 point higher?
Mental Focus	1	2	3	4	5	
Mental/Emotional/Attitude	1	2	3	4	5	
Productivity	1	2	3	4	5	
Energy	1	2	3	4	5	
Social Connections	1	2	3	4	5	

Win tomorrow today: Plan your top 3 priorities the night before or early in the morning. For each activity, ask yourself "Is there a smarter way to achieve the same outcome?"

"Productivity is less about what you do with your time. And more about how you run your mind."
— Robin S. Sharma

DAY: _____   DAILY THEME: _____

Win the Day Planning

Today, I am grateful I get to be a coach because:

I have reviewed my team, recruiting, administrative & personal goals ☐

Today's Results List: List in priority order the top 3 things you can accomplish that would make a measurable impact on your goals and projects? What metric are you trying to hit? Schedule it.

Priority #1:   **Metric I am aiming for_____**

Priority #2:   **Metric I am aiming for_____**

Priority #3:   **Metric I am aiming for_____**

○ **Morning Routine**   ○ **Workday Startup Routine**

TIME	DAILY SCHEDULE
5 am	
6 am	
7 am	
8 am	
9 am	
10 am	
11 am	
12 pm	
1 pm	
2 pm	
3 pm	
4 pm	
5 pm	
6 pm	
7 pm	
8 pm	
9 pm	
10 pm	
11 pm	

○ **Workday Shutdown Routine**   ○ **Evening Routine**

Person/People I need to Lead or Connect with Today (and How to Do It Well)

Staff meeting topics to cover:

What or Who Am I Waiting On To Get a Project Done:

Team meeting topics to cover:

Who Needs Something From Me Today or This Week That I Can Proactively Get To Them?

THE DAILY TO-DO'S

Recruiting:

Calls/texts to make:

On Campus Visits:

Events to Recruit at:

Time Spent today

Team:

Time Spent today

Administrative

Time Spent today

Social Media:

Time Spent today

Personal:

Time Spent today

PILE UP ZONE: Great ideas, goals, projects, apps or people to follow up on later

5 PERFORMANCE PILLARS	Give yourself a score of 1-5, 1=low and 5=high in terms of productivity					What could you do to get 1 point higher?
Mental Focus	1	2	3	4	5	
Mental/Emotional/Attitude	1	2	3	4	5	
Productivity	1	2	3	4	5	
Energy	1	2	3	4	5	
Social Connections	1	2	3	4	5	

Win tomorrow today: Plan your top 3 priorities the night before or early in the morning. For each activity, ask yourself "Is there a smarter way to achieve the same outcome?

"Activity leads to productivity." — Jim Rohn

4 WEEK - PLAN, DO, REVIEW, AND IMPROVE THE SYSTEM

Here is your chance to reflect back on the last month and see…

What should I/we stop doing? What should I/we do less? What should I/we continue doing? What should I/we do more? What should I/we start doing?

Reflect back on your activities to track and see your progress, notice patterns and review your accomplishments, gives you the opportunity to adjust, re-invent and plan your next 4 weeks.

The cycle is: Do the work → Look back → Look forward → Plan the next 4 weeks → Do the work…

	What Should I/We Stop Doing?	What Should I/We Do Less?	What Should I/We Continue Doing?	What Should I/we Do More Of?	What Should I/We Start Doing?
Recruiting Goals, Processes, Daily Activities					
Team Goals, Projects, Daily Activities					
Administrative Goals, Projects, Daily Activities					
Personal Goals, Projects, Daily Activities					
5 Performance Pillars					

4 WEEK SPRINT - PLAN, DO, REVIEW, AND IMPROVE THE SYSTEM

TIME AUDIT:

	Actual Time Spent	Ideal Time Spent	Adjustments to make:
Recruiting			
Team			
Administrative			
Social Media			
Personal			

3 big wins over the last 30 days were . . .

My biggest struggle over the last 30 days was. . .

. .and if I were advising or mentoring someone dealing with the same struggle, I'd advise them to . . .

4 WEEK PERFORMANCE REVIEW

Score yourself on a scale of 1 to 5 in each of the areas below, with 5 being the best. Also, write any notes in the bubbles about what is happening in that area or what you would like to improve. Be honest, but also be kind to yourself. Tally your scores up and multiply by 2, and that will give you a score out of 100. Basically, you're doing a spot check on your life and giving yourself a score so that you know where you are.

RECRUITING	ADMINISTRATIVE	TEAM/STAFF	SOCIAL MEDIA	PRODUCTIVITY
Score 1-5_____	Score 1-5_____	Score 1-5_____	Score 1-5_____	Score 1-5_____

HEALTH/ENERGY	MENTAL/EMOTIONAL	FAMILY	FRIENDS	FOCUS
Score 1-5_____	Score 1-5_____	Score 1-5_____	Score 1-5_____	Score 1-5_____

COACHING ASSESSMENT

The goal of this assessment is to help you identify areas for improvement in the major areas of your coaching life. As with any self-assessment, the goal isn't a complete snapshot of every nuance of your life, but rather a good opportunity for overall self-reflection. Don't worry about the exact wording of these descriptions. Instead, just give your overall impression of how you

HEALTH
I regularly take care of myself so that I can feel my best. I want my overall physical and emotional health to be optimized to make me feel energetic and strong each day. I strive to eat well, sleep well, and work out so that I have the physical energy and stamina to

1 2 3 4 5 6 7 8 9 10

MENTAL/EMOTIONAL
I keep a positive outlook and attitude. I take care of myself by being mindful to the energy, focus, and emotions I really want to experience and generate in life.

1 2 3 4 5 6 7 8 9 10

FAMILY
I am present with my family when I am able to be home with them. I am creating deep connection, and fun and positive energy with the family members that I keep in contact with. It's evident that I love my family and I'm doing my best for them.

1 2 3 4 5 6 7 8 9 10

FRIENDS/LIFESTYLE
I have hobbies outside of work that I enjoy and take part in a few times a week. My immediate social circle of friends bring connection, fun, and positive energy into my life. I seek out positive people and I do my best to bring positive energy and real authenticity

1 2 3 4 5 6 7 8 9 10

COACHING
I feel clear, energized, and fulfilled by my work and contributions to my team, staff, and program. I believe my work or day's effort adds real value and is a true reflection of my best efforts and contributions. I am truly engaged and excited by what I'm doing.

1 2 3 4 5 6 7 8 9 10

RECRUITING
I have a plan for how to effectively and efficiently recruiting this generation of recruits, their parents and club coaches. I am confident in selling myself, my team, program, and school. I carve out time every single week to work on recruiting and make sure I am

1 2 3 4 5 6 7 8 9 10

ADMINISTRATION
I have set up a high performance environment with yearly, quarterly, monthly, weekly, and daily methods of operation. I have systems in place to automate, delegate, or delete

1 2 3 4 5 6 7 8 9 10

TEAM/STAFF
We have a strong vision, strong leadership, and a strong culture. I am surrounded by

1 2 3 4 5 6 7 8 9 10

PRODUCTIVITY
I am successfully completing sequential steps in a timely manner that bring me closer to accomplishing important tasks, projects, or goals I have set. I am able to stay on task and still make progress even when I feel unmotivated, distracted or discouraged.

1 2 3 4 5 6 7 8 9 10

FOCUS
I am able to follow ONE course until success and remain distraction free in the process.

1 2 3 4 5 6 7 8 9 10

IDEAS TO IMPROVE ANY OF THESE AREAS INCLUDE:

TOTAL SCORE:_____

HOW TO PLAN YOUR IDEAL WEEK

Your ideal week is a planning tool. It's what your perfect week would look like if you could control 100% of what happens. The premise behind this tool is that you have a choice in life. You can either live on purpose, according to a plan that you've set or you can live by accident, reacting to the demands of others. The first approach is proactive and the second is reactive.

Now granted, you can't plan for everything. You can't control everything. Things happen that you can't anticipate, but it's a whole lot easier to accomplish what matters most when you're proactive and you begin with the end in mind. And that's where your ideal week is designed to do.

Setting up your ideal week is also important because it puts boundaries on the amount of time that you're allowed to work because we put the big rocks on the calendar first. The intention is to build your program around your life, not your life around your program.

Too many coaches find that they're working too much. It happens because there are no boundaries in place and everything for work is bleeding into their personal time. Have you ever seen a little kid bowling with the boundaries up so there were no gutter balls? I don't want you to have any gutter balls with your time. I want you to put the big rocks in place first, to create boundaries around your time.

- You'll enter first your daily theme. You're going to want to try to batch your activities based on those themes. It can be useful to batch similar activities together in order to maximize your focus and your productivity.
- When are you taking care of yourself? (working out, eating, doing personal development, sleeping)
- What family or friend obligations to do you have?
- When do you have practice, meetings, weights, etc.?I now want you to put in 3 lines.
- When do you wake up?
- When will you go to bed?
- When are you going to stop working each day? This time will help us create boundaries for how long you are going to allow yourself to work each day. Parkinson's Law states that work will expand to the time you give it. If you say you are going to work all day, you will work all day. If you give yourself less time to complete the work you need to do, you will work with more urgency and focus.

See what time you have left on your calendar. When can you block off bigger chunks of time to complete really important projects like recruiting? You will never make progress if you are just working on things a little bit here and there. Blocking off time where you have good focus, energy, and when you have the fewest distractions will set you up to successfully complete the task.

Now, keep in mind that your ideal week is just that, your ideal week. It's not going to happen every week. In fact, it might not happen most weeks, but hopefully over time you're going to be able to shape your weeks based on this model so you can become more and more focused and more and more efficient.

Once you've created your ideal week, it's good to share it with your teammates and your family. They can help you stick to your ideal week if they know what you're shooting for. If they don't know, they may inadvertently be undermining your efforts. You're going to find that this is a work in progress, so be easy on yourself. Every 90 days is a new opportunity for you to evaluate what's working, what's not, and then adjust accordingly.

YOUR IDEAL WEEK EXAMPLE

Day Themes

TIME	MONDAY	TUESDAY	WEDNESDAY
5:00 - 5:30 AM	Wake-up/ Non-urgent Important	Wake-up/ Non-urgent Important	Wake-up/ Non-urgent Important
6:00 - 6:30 AM	Jack getting ready for school	Jack getting ready for school	Jack getting ready for school
7:00 - 7:30 AM	Non-Urgent Important Work	Non-Urgent Important Work	Non-Urgent Important Work
8:00 - 8:30 AM	Ashleigh to School/walk the dogs	Ashleigh to School/walk the dogs	Ashleigh to School/walk the dogs
9:00 - 9:30 AM	Work	Work	Work
10:00 - 10:30 AM			
11:00 - 11:30 AM			
12:00 - 12:30 PM			
1:00 - 1:30 PM			
2:00 - 2:30 PM			
3:00 - 3:30 PM	Kids home from school	Kids home from school	Kids home from school
4:00 - 4:30 PM			
5:00 - 5:30 PM	Workout		Workout
6:00 - 6:30 PM	Family Dinner	Family Dinner	Family Dinner
7:00 - 7:30 PM	Martial Arts	Martial Arts	Martial Arts
8:00 - 8:30 PM	Reverse Alarm		
9:00 - 9:30 PM	Bedtime		
10:00 - 10:30 PM			
11:00 - 11:30 PM			
12:00 - 12:30 AM			

Focus Areas

THURSDAY	FRIDAY	SATURDAY	SUNDAY
Wake-up/ Non-urgent Important	Wake-up/ Non-urgent Important	Wake-up/ Non-urgent Important	Wake-up/ Non-urgent Important
Jack getting ready for school	Jack getting ready for school	Work	Weekly Review
Non-Urgent Important Work	Non-Urgent Important Work		Planning Time
Ashleigh to School/walk the dogs	Ashleigh to School/walk the dogs		Device Free
Work	Work		
		Family Time	
Kids home from school	Kids home from school		Family Time
Workout	Ninja Warrior for Jack		
Family Dinner	Family Dinner	Family Dinner	Family Dinner
Martial Arts			

YOUR IDEAL WEEK

1.

⭘

2.

⭘

3.

⭘

Make time for what matters first.

Note on this calendar when you will have:

1. Family time
2. Weekly reflection
3. Self-care time
4. Wake up time
5. Go to bed time
6. Work stop time
7. Practice
8. Weights
9. Meetings
10. After all of this is set, what big blocks of time to do you have left for the growth and improvement projects you listed above? Find at least 1 hour each day and block it off.
11. Fit all of the busy work in between your blocks of program building projects.

Day Themes

TIME	MONDAY	TUESDAY	WEDNESDAY
5:00 - 5:30 AM			
6:00 - 6:30 AM			
7:00 - 7:30 AM			
8:00 - 8:30 AM			
9:00 - 9:30 AM			
10:00 - 10:30 AM			
11:00 - 11:30 AM			
12:00 - 12:30 PM			
1:00 - 1:30 PM			
2:00 - 2:30 PM			
3:00 - 3:30 PM			
4:00 - 4:30 PM			
5:00 - 5:30 PM			
6:00 - 6:30 PM			
7:00 - 7:30 PM			
8:00 - 8:30 PM			
9:00 - 9:30 PM			
10:00 - 10:30 PM			
11:00 - 11:30 PM			
12:00 - 12:30 AM			

Last week's wins & lessons learned:

USE THIS PAGE TO CREATE AN OVERVIEW FOR NEXT WEEK

THURSDAY	FRIDAY	SATURDAY	SUNDAY

Thoughts for this upcoming week:

YOUR IDEAL WEEK

FOCUS AREA FOR GROWTH AND IMPROVEMENT THIS WEEK	✓
1.	○
2.	○
3.	○

Focus Areas

Day Themes

TIME	MONDAY	TUESDAY	WEDNESDAY
5:00 - 5:30 AM			
6:00 - 6:30 AM			
7:00 - 7:30 AM			
8:00 - 8:30 AM			
9:00 - 9:30 AM			
10:00 - 10:30 AM			
11:00 - 11:30 AM			
12:00 - 12:30 PM			
1:00 - 1:30 PM			
2:00 - 2:30 PM			
3:00 - 3:30 PM			
4:00 - 4:30 PM			
5:00 - 5:30 PM			
6:00 - 6:30 PM			
7:00 - 7:30 PM			
8:00 - 8:30 PM			
9:00 - 9:30 PM			
10:00 - 10:30 PM			
11:00 - 11:30 PM			
12:00 - 12:30 AM			

HOW TO SCHEDULE YOUR IDEAL WEEK

Make time for what matters first.

Note on this calendar when you will have:

1. Family time
2. Weekly reflection
3. Self-care time
4. Wake up time
5. Go to bed time
6. Work stop time
7. Practice
8. Weights
9. Meetings
10. After all of this is set, what big blocks of time to do you have left for the growth and improvement projects you listed above? Find at least 1 hour each day and block it off.
11. Fit all of the busy work in between your blocks of program building projects.

Last week's wins & lessons learned:

USE THIS PAGE TO CREATE AN OVERVIEW FOR NEXT WEEK

THURSDAY	FRIDAY	SATURDAY	SUNDAY

Thoughts for this upcoming week:

YOUR IDEAL WEEK

	FOCUS AREA FOR GROWTH AND IMPROVEMENT THIS WEEK	✓
1.		○
2.		○
3.		○

Focus Areas

TIME	MONDAY	TUESDAY	WEDNESDAY
5:00 - 5:30 AM			
6:00 - 6:30 AM			
7:00 - 7:30 AM			
8:00 - 8:30 AM			
9:00 - 9:30 AM			
10:00 - 10:30 AM			
11:00 - 11:30 AM			
12:00 - 12:30 PM			
1:00 - 1:30 PM			
2:00 - 2:30 PM			
3:00 - 3:30 PM			
4:00 - 4:30 PM			
5:00 - 5:30 PM			
6:00 - 6:30 PM			
7:00 - 7:30 PM			
8:00 - 8:30 PM			
9:00 - 9:30 PM			
10:00 - 10:30 PM			
11:00 - 11:30 PM			
12:00 - 12:30 AM			

HOW TO SCHEDULE YOUR IDEAL WEEK

Make time for what matters first.

Note on this calendar when you will have:

1. Family time
2. Weekly reflection
3. Self-care time
4. Wake up time
5. Go to bed time
6. Work stop time
7. Practice
8. Weights
9. Meetings
10. After all of this is set, what big blocks of time to do you have left for the growth and improvement projects you listed above? Find at least 1 hour each day and block it off.
11. Fit all of the busy work in between your blocks of program building projects.

Last week's wins & lessons learned:

USE THIS PAGE TO CREATE AN OVERVIEW FOR NEXT WEEK

THURSDAY	FRIDAY	SATURDAY	SUNDAY

Thoughts for this upcoming week:

YOUR IDEAL WEEK

	FOCUS AREA FOR GROWTH AND IMPROVEMENT THIS WEEK	✓
1.		
		○
2.		
		○
3.		
		○

Focus Areas

TIME	MONDAY	TUESDAY	WEDNESDAY
5:00 - 5:30 AM			
6:00 - 6:30 AM			
7:00 - 7:30 AM			
8:00 - 8:30 AM			
9:00 - 9:30 AM			
10:00 - 10:30 AM			
11:00 - 11:30 AM			
12:00 - 12:30 PM			
1:00 - 1:30 PM			
2:00 - 2:30 PM			
3:00 - 3:30 PM			
4:00 - 4:30 PM			
5:00 - 5:30 PM			
6:00 - 6:30 PM			
7:00 - 7:30 PM			
8:00 - 8:30 PM			
9:00 - 9:30 PM			
10:00 - 10:30 PM			
11:00 - 11:30 PM			
12:00 - 12:30 AM			

HOW TO SCHEDULE YOUR IDEAL WEEK

Make time for what matters first.

Note on this calendar when you will have:

1. Family time
2. Weekly reflection
3. Self-care time
4. Wake up time
5. Go to bed time
6. Work stop time
7. Practice
8. Weights
9. Meetings
10. After all of this is set, what big blocks of time to do you have left for the growth and improvement projects you listed above? Find at least 1 hour each day and block it off.
11. Fit all of the busy work in between your blocks of program building projects.

Last week's wins & lessons learned:

USE THIS PAGE TO CREATE AN OVERVIEW FOR NEXT WEEK

THURSDAY	FRIDAY	SATURDAY	SUNDAY

Thoughts for this upcoming week:

YOUR IDEAL WEEK

Focus Areas

Day Themes

TIME	MONDAY	TUESDAY	WEDNESDAY
5:00 - 5:30 AM			
6:00 - 6:30 AM			
7:00 - 7:30 AM			
8:00 - 8:30 AM			
9:00 - 9:30 AM			
10:00 - 10:30 AM			
11:00 - 11:30 AM			
12:00 - 12:30 PM			
1:00 - 1:30 PM			
2:00 - 2:30 PM			
3:00 - 3:30 PM			
4:00 - 4:30 PM			
5:00 - 5:30 PM			
6:00 - 6:30 PM			
7:00 - 7:30 PM			
8:00 - 8:30 PM			
9:00 - 9:30 PM			
10:00 - 10:30 PM			
11:00 - 11:30 PM			
12:00 - 12:30 AM			

HOW TO SCHEDULE YOUR IDEAL WEEK

Make time for what matters first.

Note on this calendar when you will have:

1. Family time
2. Weekly reflection
3. Self-care time
4. Wake up time
5. Go to bed time
6. Work stop time
7. Practice
8. Weights
9. Meetings
10. After all of this is set, what big blocks of time to do you have left for the growth and improvement projects you listed above? Find at least 1 hour each day and block it off.
11. Fit all of the busy work in between your blocks of program building projects.

Last week's wins & lessons learned:

USE THIS PAGE TO CREATE AN OVERVIEW FOR NEXT WEEK

THURSDAY	FRIDAY	SATURDAY	SUNDAY

Thoughts for this upcoming week:

4 WEEK - PLAN, DO, REVIEW, AND IMPROVE THE SYSTEM

Here is your chance to reflect back on the last month and see...

What should I/we stop doing? What should I/we do less? What should I/we continue doing? What should I/we do more? What should I/we start doing?

Reflect back on your activities to track and see your progress, notice patterns and review your accomplishments, gives you the opportunity to adjust, re-invent and plan your next 4 weeks.

The cycle is: Do the work → Look back → Look forward → Plan the next 4 weeks → Do the work...

	What Should I/We Stop Doing?	What Should I/We Do Less?	What Should I/We Continue Doing?	What Should I/we Do More Of?	What Should I/We Start Doing?
Recruiting Goals, Processes, Daily Activities					
Team Goals, Projects, Daily Activities					
Administrative Goals, Projects, Daily Activities					
Personal Goals, Projects, Daily Activities					
5 Performance Pillars					

4 WEEK SPRINT - PLAN, DO, REVIEW, AND IMPROVE THE SYSTEM

TIME AUDIT:

	Actual Time Spent	Ideal Time Spent	Adjustments to make:
Recruiting			
Team			
Administrative			
Social Media			
Personal			

3 big wins over the last 30 days were . . .

My biggest struggle over the last 30 days was. . .

. .and if I were advising or mentoring someone dealing with the same struggle, I'd advise them to . . .

4 WEEK PERFORMANCE REVIEW

Score yourself on a scale of 1 to 5 in each of the areas below, with 5 being the best. Also, write any notes in the bubbles about what is happening in that area or what you would like to improve. Be honest, but also be kind to yourself. Tally your scores up and multiply by 2, and that will give you a score out of 100. Basically, you're doing a spot check on your life and giving yourself a score so that you know where you are.

RECRUITING	ADMINISTRATIVE	TEAM/STAFF	SOCIAL MEDIA	PRODUCTIVITY
Score 1-5_____	Score 1-5_____	Score 1-5_____	Score 1-5_____	Score 1-5_____

HEALTH/ENERGY	MENTAL/EMOTIONAL	FAMILY	FRIENDS	FOCUS
Score 1-5_____	Score 1-5_____	Score 1-5_____	Score 1-5_____	Score 1-5_____

2 WEEK - PLAN, DO, REVIEW, AND IMPROVE THE SYSTEM

Here is your chance to reflect back on the next couple of weeks and see…

What should I/we stop doing? What should I/we do less? What should I/we continue doing? What should I/we do more? What should I/we start doing?

	What Should I/We Stop Doing?	What Should I/We Do Less?
Recruiting Goals, Processes, Daily Activities		
Team Goals, Projects, Daily Activities		
Administrative Goals, Projects, Daily Activities		
Personal Goals, Projects, Daily Activities		
5 Performance Pillars		

2 WEEK - PLAN, DO, REVIEW, AND IMPROVE THE SYSTEM

Reflecting back on your activities to track and see your progress, notice patterns and review your accomplishments, gives you the opportunity to adjust, re-invent and plan your next 2 weeks.

The cycle is: **Do the work** → **Look back** → **Look forward** → **Plan the next 2 weeks** → **Do the work…**

	What Should I/We Continue Doing?	What Should I/we Do More?	What Should I/We Start Doing?
Recruiting Goals, Processes, Daily Activities			
Team Goals, Projects, Daily Activities			
Administrative Goals, Projects, Daily Activities			
Personal Goals, Projects, Daily Activities			
5 Performance Pillars			

2 WEEK SPRINT - PLAN, DO, REVIEW, AND IMPROVE THE SYSTEM

TIME AUDIT:

	Actual Time Spent	Ideal Time Spent	Adjustments to make:
Recruiting			
Team			
Administrative			
Social Media			
Personal			

3 big wins over the last 14 days were . . .

My biggest struggle over the last 14 days was. . .

. .and if I were advising or mentoring someone dealing with the same struggle, I'd advise them to . . .

2 WEEK PERFORMANCE REVIEW

Score yourself on a scale of 1 to 5 in each of the areas below, with 5 being the best. Also, write any notes in the bubbles about what is happening in that area or what you would like to improve. Be honest, but also be kind to yourself. Tally your scores up and multiply by 2, and that will give you a score out of 100. Basically, you're doing a spot check on your life and

RECRUITING	ADMINISTRATIVE	TEAM/STAFF	SOCIAL MEDIA	PRODUCTIVITY
Score 1-5_____	Score 1-5_____	Score 1-5_____	Score 1-5_____	Score 1-5_____

HEALTH/ENERGY	MENTAL/EMOTIONAL	FAMILY	FRIENDS	FOCUS
Score 1-5_____	Score 1-5_____	Score 1-5_____	Score 1-5_____	Score 1-5_____

Success is not a result of heroic feats, grand acts of bravery or quantum leaps. Success is a result of small, seemingly innocuous moment-to-moment choices.

-Darren Hardy

YOUR IDEAL WEEK

<table>
<tr><th></th><th>FOCUS AREA FOR GROWTH AND IMPROVEMENT THIS WEEK</th><th>✓</th></tr>
</table>

FOCUS AREA FOR GROWTH AND IMPROVEMENT THIS WEEK	✓
1.	
	○
2.	
	○
3.	
	○

Focus Areas

HOW TO SCHEDULE YOUR IDEAL WEEK

Make time for what matters first.

Note on this calendar when you will have:

1. Family time
2. Weekly reflection
3. Self-care time
4. Wake up time
5. Go to bed time
6. Work stop time
7. Practice
8. Weights
9. Meetings
10. After all of this is set, what big blocks of time to do you have left for the growth and improvement projects you listed above? Find at least 1 hour each day and block it off.
11. Fit all of the busy work in between your blocks of program building projects.

TIME	MONDAY	TUESDAY	WEDNESDAY
5:00 - 5:30 AM			
6:00 - 6:30 AM			
7:00 - 7:30 AM			
8:00 - 8:30 AM			
9:00 - 9:30 AM			
10:00 - 10:30 AM			
11:00 - 11:30 AM			
12:00 - 12:30 PM			
1:00 - 1:30 PM			
2:00 - 2:30 PM			
3:00 - 3:30 PM			
4:00 - 4:30 PM			
5:00 - 5:30 PM			
6:00 - 6:30 PM			
7:00 - 7:30 PM			
8:00 - 8:30 PM			
9:00 - 9:30 PM			
10:00 - 10:30 PM			
11:00 - 11:30 PM			
12:00 - 12:30 AM			

Last week's wins & lessons learned:

USE THIS PAGE TO CREATE AN OVERVIEW FOR NEXT WEEK

THURSDAY	FRIDAY	SATURDAY	SUNDAY

Thoughts for this upcoming week:

YOUR IDEAL WEEK

Focus Areas

Day Themes

TIME	MONDAY	TUESDAY	WEDNESDAY
5:00 - 5:30 AM			
6:00 - 6:30 AM			
7:00 - 7:30 AM			
8:00 - 8:30 AM			
9:00 - 9:30 AM			
10:00 - 10:30 AM			
11:00 - 11:30 AM			
12:00 - 12:30 PM			
1:00 - 1:30 PM			
2:00 - 2:30 PM			
3:00 - 3:30 PM			
4:00 - 4:30 PM			
5:00 - 5:30 PM			
6:00 - 6:30 PM			
7:00 - 7:30 PM			
8:00 - 8:30 PM			
9:00 - 9:30 PM			
10:00 - 10:30 PM			
11:00 - 11:30 PM			
12:00 - 12:30 AM			

Last week's wins & lessons learned:

USE THIS PAGE TO CREATE AN OVERVIEW FOR NEXT WEEK

THURSDAY	FRIDAY	SATURDAY	SUNDAY

Thoughts for this upcoming week:

YOUR IDEAL WEEK

Focus Areas

HOW TO SCHEDULE YOUR IDEAL WEEK

Make time for what matters first.

Note on this calendar when you will have:

1. Family time
2. Weekly reflection
3. Self-care time
4. Wake up time
5. Go to bed time
6. Work stop time
7. Practice
8. Weights
9. Meetings
10. After all of this is set, what big blocks of time to do you have left for the growth and improvement projects you listed above? Find at least 1 hour each day and block it off.
11. Fit all of the busy work in between your blocks of program building projects.

Day Themes

TIME	MONDAY	TUESDAY	WEDNESDAY
5:00 - 5:30 AM			
6:00 - 6:30 AM			
7:00 - 7:30 AM			
8:00 - 8:30 AM			
9:00 - 9:30 AM			
10:00 - 10:30 AM			
11:00 - 11:30 AM			
12:00 - 12:30 PM			
1:00 - 1:30 PM			
2:00 - 2:30 PM			
3:00 - 3:30 PM			
4:00 - 4:30 PM			
5:00 - 5:30 PM			
6:00 - 6:30 PM			
7:00 - 7:30 PM			
8:00 - 8:30 PM			
9:00 - 9:30 PM			
10:00 - 10:30 PM			
11:00 - 11:30 PM			
12:00 - 12:30 AM			

Last week's wins & lessons learned:

USE THIS PAGE TO CREATE AN OVERVIEW FOR NEXT WEEK

THURSDAY	FRIDAY	SATURDAY	SUNDAY

Thoughts for this upcoming week:

YOUR IDEAL WEEK

Focus Areas

HOW TO SCHEDULE YOUR IDEAL WEEK

Make time for what matters first.

Note on this calendar when you will have:

1. Family time
2. Weekly reflection
3. Self-care time
4. Wake up time
5. Go to bed time
6. Work stop time
7. Practice
8. Weights
9. Meetings
10. After all of this is set, what big blocks of time to do you have left for the growth and improvement projects you listed above? Find at least 1 hour each day and block it off.
11. Fit all of the busy work in between your blocks of program building projects.

Day Themes

TIME	MONDAY	TUESDAY	WEDNESDAY
5:00 - 5:30 AM			
6:00 - 6:30 AM			
7:00 - 7:30 AM			
8:00 - 8:30 AM			
9:00 - 9:30 AM			
10:00 - 10:30 AM			
11:00 - 11:30 AM			
12:00 - 12:30 PM			
1:00 - 1:30 PM			
2:00 - 2:30 PM			
3:00 - 3:30 PM			
4:00 - 4:30 PM			
5:00 - 5:30 PM			
6:00 - 6:30 PM			
7:00 - 7:30 PM			
8:00 - 8:30 PM			
9:00 - 9:30 PM			
10:00 - 10:30 PM			
11:00 - 11:30 PM			
12:00 - 12:30 AM			

Last week's wins & lessons learned:

USE THIS PAGE TO CREATE AN OVERVIEW FOR NEXT WEEK

THURSDAY	FRIDAY	SATURDAY	SUNDAY

Thoughts for this upcoming week:

365 Day Social Media System for Coaches Online Course

Want your social media campaign to do more than simply create a presence online but to actually drive your recruiting success. Get an interview done by Dan Tudor on how social media can be used effectively to help with your recruiting. Get a step-by-step process, checklists, and social media scorecards.

Recruiting Made Simple.

If you want ongoing training on how to make the process of recruiting more simple, consider joining this group. We meet once a month and go in depth on 1 topic. You get my worksheets, checklists, and templates. You also can get 1-on-1 implementation calls with me. Click here for the Recruiting Made Simple details.

Win the Day Academy Online Course

Mandy hosted a unique coaching group that helped the students reduce chaos, get organized and build stable programs run on systems and processes. She covered all of the questions and addressed all of the problems coaches like you have been talking to her all year!

Get 1 on 1 or staff coaching By Mandy Green

Mandy will help you, or include you in a small group of coaches, through their busy coaching lives and help set a game plan to recruit and organize your schedule to help you do what you want to do most: coach and spend time with family! Set up a call with me by emailing me at mandy@busy.coach.

30-Day Productivity Habits for Coaches

Want to separate yourself from the competition? Take this 30-Day Productivity Habit

Challenge to learn habits and triggers that the most successful in their field use.

Kick-Ass Recruiting Workbook

Set the course for an incredible year of recruiting success and accomplishment using these simple exercises that help you create clarity, get organized and become laser focused on your key recruiting activities.

Busy Coach Daily Planner

Get the recruits you want in the most effective way. Daily social media and recruiting planner for college coaches. Be able to plan your year, design & execute your days and keep your priorities in clear view to achieve what matters in recruiting your championship team everyday.

Busy Coach Tracking Journal

Don't leave your success to chance. Learn how to effectively track and measure results in key performance areas of your coaching life to reduce stress, improve daily execution and reduce time sucking activities.

Time-Management Workbook for Coaches

FINALLY! A college coach-specific how-to guide that is going to walk through how to plan and organize your coaching life and help you 10X your productivity.

Printed in the United States
by Baker & Taylor Publisher Services